# SAMUEL PEPYS' DIARY

In this book, for the first time, the entries in *Samuel Pepys' Diary* are selected and arranged to be read and enjoyed by the person with limited leisure. The editor has concentrated and emphasized the points of high interest. The copious index, at the same time, provides guidance for the scholarly reader who desires to study the *Diary* for its more subtle hints of the life and times of the writer.

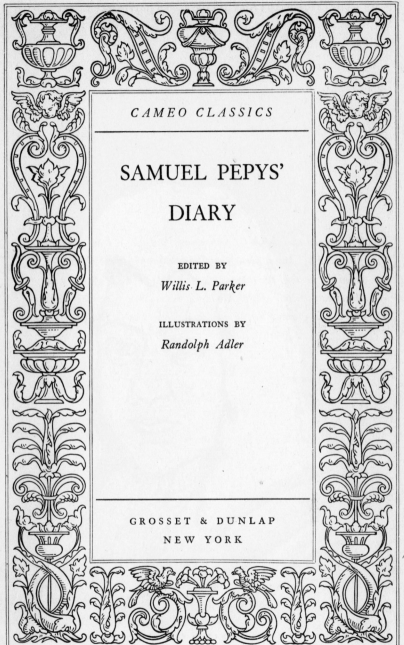

CAMEO CLASSICS

# SAMUEL PEPYS'
# DIARY

EDITED BY

*Willis L. Parker*

ILLUSTRATIONS BY

*Randolph Adler*

GROSSET & DUNLAP
NEW YORK

*The cameo of Johann Gutenberg on the cover is from a medal produced by Anton Scharff, of Vienna, for the late Robert Hoe, from the head of the famous portrait statue of Gutenberg by the American sculptor, Ralph Goddard. Permission to use the medal was granted by the owner, William Edwin Rudge.*

PRINTED IN THE UNITED STATES OF AMERICA
BY J. J. LITTLE AND IVES COMPANY, NEW YORK

# PREFACE

## PREFACE

SCHOLARS and editors who have prepared the Pepys *Diary* for publication have in the past customarily indulged themselves in profuse introductions. In this book will be no such thing. A few plain, brief statements are all the reader needs to prepare him for reading and enjoying the Diary.

As to the diarist: Samuel Pepys (pronounced *Peps* or *Peeps*) was born on February 23rd, **1633.** He was of a rather well-known country family. His character, diligence, and a distant relationship brought him to the attention of Edward Montagu, a friend of Oliver Cromwell, and when Montagu, for his assistance at the Restoration of Charles II, was made Earl of Sandwich, he obtained for Pepys the position of Clerk of the Acts to the Navy Board. Promotions followed from this, and Pepys grew wealthy and was held in high respect. He had married in 1655 Elizabeth, daughter of one Alexander St. Michel, a Huguenot exile from France.

As to the *Diary*: What impelled Pepys to keep this *Diary* is not for knowledge but speculation. The *Diary* was undoubtedly a secret; during his lifetime, seemingly, Pepys mentioned its existence only to one man, Sir W. Coventry. He kept it in shorthand, and when his eyes failed after nine and one-half years of meticulous regularity in his daily entries, he broke off altogether. If any other man ever kept such a *Diary,* it is unknown. Perhaps none has ever felt the assurance Pepys seems to have had that its decipherment would be long deferred. No such naïve record of ordinary daily doings is known. It is safe to predict that none of us will ever be given such an opportunity to appraise our most intimate friends as we can measure Pepys from this record. Opinions and speculations about it are infinite in number and possibility, and none will be offered here. The reader can and must speculate for himself.

As to the historical background: When the *Diary* opens, the Commonwealth is near an end and the Restoration of Charles II is under way, to be accomplished within six months. The *Diary* continues into the ninth year of the King's reign. Two major calamities, besides a disastrous war with the Dutch, occurred in this interval: The Plague visited London and killed its thousands, and the great fire of 1666 almost destroyed the city. Details beyond these can be had from any brief history of England.*

As to this book: This is one volume, amounting to about two hundred pages, all told. The complete *Diary* fills eight volumes, in smaller type than we use. Given the leisure, one can enjoy the reading of the complete *Diary,* allowing the memory to recall incidents pertinent to the one of the moment's perusing. Thus is Pepys to be read with the greatest enjoyment. However, the greater number of us have not and

---

* A good one is *A Short History of the English People,* J. R. Green, which is available in many editions.

will not ever have the leisure to read and digest an eight-volume book. Because of that, many abridged editions of Pepys have been published, all of them, by the editors' confessions, mere tastes from the edge of the dish, crumbs from the table. It has seemed to the present editor that if we must eat crumbs it would be pleasant to have them served as a banquet is served, and this is what has been here attempted. In this book it is hoped that the fine savor of the Seventeenth Century can be seized by the person with minutes for reading, as heretofore it has been possible only to the person with hours for his library. The judgment is with the reader.

W. L. PARKER.

New York,
March 18th, 1932.

## THE DIARY OF SAMUEL PEPYS

*P**EPYS** began his diary January 1st, 1660, about two months before his twenty-seventh birthday. The date was in a critical period of English history; Oliver Cromwell had been dead fifteen months, and the English people were growing tired of the experiment of the Commonwealth, the more so as Oliver's son and successor was every day more obviously and hopelessly inadequate to his powers and responsibilities.—*EDITOR.

Blessed be God, at the end of the last year I was in very good health, without any sense of my old pain, but upon taking of cold. I lived in Axe Yard, having my wife and servant Jane, and no more in family than us three. My wife gave me hopes of her being with child, but on the last day of the year the hope was belied.

The condition of the State was thus: viz. the Rump, after being disturbed by my Lord Lambert, was lately returned to sit again. The officers of the Army all forced to yield. Lawson lies still in the river, and Monk is with his army in Scotland. The new Common Council of the City do speak very high; and had sent to Monk their swordbearer, to acquaint him with their desires for a free and full Parliament, which is at present the desires, and the hopes, and expectation of all. My own private condition very handsome, and esteemed rich, but indeed very poor; besides my goods of my house, and my office, which at present is somewhat uncertain. Mr. Downing master of my office.

JANUARY 1ST (Lord's Day).* This morning (we living lately in the garret) I rose, put on my suit with great skirts, having not lately worn any other clothes but them. Went to Mr. Gunning's chapel at Exeter House, where he made a very good sermon upon these words:—"That in the fulness of time God sent his Son, made of a woman, &c."; showing, that by "made under the law," is meant his circumcision, which is solemnized this day. Dined at home in the garret, where my wife dressed the remains of a turkey, and in the doing of it she burned her hand. I staid at home all the afternoon, looking over my accounts.

* This is the Old Style calendar. The Gregorian correction had not been accepted in England.

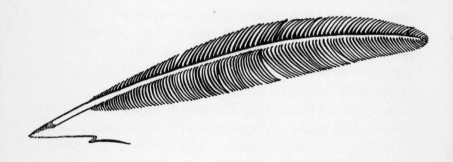

## ENGLAND REPUDIATES THE COMMONWEALTH

JANUARY 17TH, 1660. Home and wrote by the Post, and carried to Whitehall, and coming back turned in at Harper's, where Jack Price was, and I drank with him and he told me among other things how much the Protector* is altered; though he would seem to bear out his trouble very well, yet he is scarce able to talk sense with a man.

FEBRUARY 27TH. Up by four o'clock, and after I was ready, Mr. Blayton and I took horse and straight to Saffron Walden, where at the White Hart we set up our horses, and took the master of the house to shew us Audley End House, who took us on foot through the park, and so to the house, where the housekeeper shewed us all the house, in which the stateliness of the ceilings, chimney-pieces, and form of the whole was exceedingly worth seeing. He took us into the cellar, where we drank most admirable drink, a health to the King.

MARCH 2ND. This morning I went early to my Lord at Mr. Crew's where I spoke to him. Here were a great many come to see him, as Secretary Thurlow who is now by this Parliament chosen again Secretary of State. There were also General

---

* Richard Cromwell, who succeeded Oliver.

Monk's trumpeters to give my Lord a sound of their trumpets this morning. Thence I went to my office and wrote a letter to Mr. Downing about the business of his house. Great is the talk of a single person, and that it would now be Charles, George, or Richard again.* For the last of which, my Lord St. John is said to speak high. Great also is the dispute now in the House, in whose name the writs shall run for the next Parliament; and it is said that Mr. Prin, in open House, said, "In King Charles's."

MARCH 5TH. We drank till Mr. Adams began to be overcome. Then we parted, and so to Westminster by water, only seeing Mr. Pinkney at his own house, where he shewed me how he had alway kept the Lion and Unicorn, in the back of his chimney, bright, in expectation of the King's coming again. At home I found Mr. Hunt, who told me how the Parliament had voted that the Covenant be printed and hung in churches again. Great hopes of the King's coming again. To bed.

*Though a Royalist sympathizer, Pepys was not of the inner circle. His patron Sir Edward Montagu, however, was a powerful and influential man. Sir Edward was chosen General at Sea on February 29th, and a deputation was arranged to be sent to Charles in Holland, in the hope or expectation that Parliament would invite him to return to the throne. Sir Edward was among the leaders of this deputation.—EDITOR.*

MARCH 6TH (Shrove Tuesday). I called Mr. Sheply and we both went up to my Lord's lodgings at Mr. Crew's, where he

* The Parliament wished to put the government of the realm into one man's hands, whether he were Charles Stuart, George Monk or Richard Cromwell. As history developed, of course, Monk threw his influence to Charles Stuart and the latter became King.

bade us to go home again, and get a fire against an hour after. Which we did at White Hall, whither he came, and after talking with him and me about his going to sea, he called me by myself to go along with him into the garden, where he asked me how things were with me, and what he had endeavoured to do with my uncle to get him to do something for me but he would say nothing too. He likewise bade me look out now at this turn some good place, and he would use all his own, and all the interest of his friends that he had in England, to do me good. And asked me whether I could, without too much inconvenience, go to sea as his secretary, and bid me think of it. He told me also, that he did believe the King would come in, and did discourse with me about it, and about the affection of the people and City, at which I was full glad.

I left him and went up to my office. Here comes my uncle Tom, whom I took to Will's and drank with; poor man, he comes to inquire about the knights of Windsor, of which he desires to get to be one. While we were drinking, in comes Mr. Day, a carpenter in Westminster, to tell me that it was Shrove Tuesday, and that I must go with him to their yearly Club upon this day, which I confess I had quite forgot. So I went to the Bell, where were Mr. Eglin, Veezy, Vincent a butcher, one more, and Mr. Tanner, with whom I played upon a viall, and he a viallin, after dinner, and were very merry, with a special good dinner, a leg of veal and bacon, two capons, and sausages and fritters, with abundance of wine. After that I went home, where I found Kate Sterpin. She gone, I went to see Mrs. Jem, at whose chamber door I found a couple of ladies, but she not being there, we hunted her out, and found that she and another had hid themselves behind a door. Well, they all went down into the dining-room, where it was full of tag, rag and bobtail, dancing, singing, and drinking, of which I was ashamed; and after I had staid a dance or two I went away. This day I hear that the Lords do intend to sit, and great store of them are now in town, and I see in the Hall to-day. My Lord told me that there was great endeavours to bring in the Protector again; but he told me too that he did believe it would not last long if he were brought in; no, nor the King neither (though he seems to think that he will come in), unless he carry himself very soberly and well. Every body now drinks the King's health without any fear, whereas before it was very private that a man dare do it. Monk this day is feasted at Mercer's Hall, and is invited one after another to all the twelve halls in London. Many think that he is honest yet, and some or more think him to be a fool that would raise himself, but think that he will undo himself by endeavouring it. My mind, I needs must remember, has been very much eased and joyed at my Lord's great expressions of kindness this day, and in discourse thereupon my wife and I lay awake an hour or two in our bed.

*Pepys decided to go to sea as secretary to Sir Edward Montagu. Six weeks later, affairs have progressed.*—EDITOR.

APRIL 18TH. I all the afternoon dictating in my cabin (my own head being troubled with multiplicity of business) to Burr, who wrote for me above a dozen letters, by which I have made my mind more light and clear than I have had it yet since I came on board. At night sent a packet to London, and

Mr. Cook returned hence bringing me this news, that the Sectaries do talk high what they will do, but I believe all to no purpose; but the Cavaliers are something unwise to talk so high on the other side as they do. That it is evident now that the General and the Council do resolve to make way for the King's coming. And it is now clear that either the Fanatiques must now be undone, or the gentry and citizens throughout England, and clergy, must fall, in spite of their militia and army, which is not at all possible I think. After that to bed, and W. Howe sat by my bed-side, and he and I sang a psalm or two and so I to sleep.

APRIL 21ST. This day dined Sir John Boys and some other gentlemen formerly great Cavaliers, and among the rest one Mr. Norwood, for whom my Lord gave a convoy to carry him to the Brill,* but he is certainly going to the King, for my Lord commanded me that I should not enter his name in my book. My Lord do show them and that sort of people great civility. All their discourse and others are of the King's coming, and we begin to speak of it very freely. And heard how in London they have set up the King's arms. In the afternoon the Captain would by all means have me up to his cabin, and there treated me huge nobly, giving me a barrel of pickled oysters, and opened another for me, and a bottle of wine, which was a very great favour.

MAY 2ND. In the morning at a breakfast of radishes at the Purser's cabin. After that to writing till dinner. At which time comes Dunne from London, with letters that tell us the welcome news of the Parliament's votes yesterday, which will be remembered for the happiest May-day that hath been many

* A seaport of Holland.

a year to England. The King's letter was read in the House, wherein he submits himself and all things to them, as to an Act of Oblivion to all, unless they shall please to except any, as to the confirming of the sales of the King's and Church lands, if they see good. The House upon reading the letter, ordered £50,000 to be forthwith provided to send to His Majesty for his present supply; and a committee chosen to return an answer of thanks to His Majesty for his gracious letter, and that the letter be kept among the records of the Parliament, and in all this not so much as one No. The City of London do disclaim any government but that of a King, Lords, and Commons. Great joy all yesterday at London, and at night more bonfires than ever, and ringing of bells, and drinking of the King's health upon their knees in the streets, which methinks is a little too much. But every body seems to be very joyfull in the business, insomuch that our sea-commanders now begin to say so too, which a week ago they would not do. And our seamen, as many as had money or credit for drink, did do nothing else this evening.

MAY 3RD. This morning my Lord showed me the King's declaration and his letter to the two Generals to be communicated to the fleet. Upon the receipt of it this morning by an express (Mr. Phillips, one of the messengers of the Council from General Monk), my Lord summoned a council of war, and in the mean time did dictate to me how he would have the vote ordered which he would have pass this council. Which done, the Commanders all came on board, and the council sat in the coach (the first council of war that had been in my time), where I read the letter and declaration; and

while they were discoursing upon it, I seemed to draw up a
vote, which being offered, they passed. Not one man seemed to
say no to it, though I am confident many in their hearts were
against it. After this was done I went up to the quarter-deck
with my Lord and the Commanders, and there read both the
papers and the vote; which done, and demanding their opinion, the seamen did all of them cry out, "God bless King
Charles!" with the greatest joy imaginable. This done and
finished my Proclamation, I returned to the Nazeby, where
my Lord was much pleased to hear how all the fleet took it
in a transport of joy, showed me a private letter of the King's
to him, and another from the Duke of York in such familiar
style as to their common friend, with all kindness imaginable.
And I found by the letters, and so my Lord told me too, that
there had been many letters passed between them for a great
while, and I perceive unknown to Monk. And among the rest
that had carried these letters, Sir John Boys is one. The King
speaks of his being courted to come to the Hague, but do
desire my Lord's advice whither to come to take ship. And
the Duke offers to learn the seaman's trade of him, in such
familiar words as if Jack Cole and I had writ them. This was
very strange to me, that my Lord should carry all things so
wisely and prudently as he do, and I was over joyful to see
him in so good condition, and he did not a little please himself
to tell me how he had provided for himself so great a hold
on the King.

After this to supper, and then to writing of letters till
twelve at night, and so up again at three in the morning. My
Lord seemed to put great confidence in me, and would take

my advice in many things. I perceive his being willing to do all the honour in the world to Monk, and to let him have all the honour of doing the business, though he will many times express his thoughts of him to be but a thick-sculled fool. So that I do believe there is some agreement more than ordinary between the King and my Lord to let Monk carry on the business, for it is he that must do the business, or at least that can hinder it, if he be not flattered and observed. This my Lord will hint himself sometimes.

*In such manner as this above, Pepys narrates the return of the King. We lack space to print it all, but there is one more deliciously pertinent item.*—EDITOR.

NOVEMBER 1ST. This morning Sir W. Pen and I were mounted early, and came to Sir W. Batten's, where he lives like a prince, and we were made very welcome. Here dined with us two or three more country gentlemen; among the rest Mr. Christmas, my old school-fellow, with whom I had much talk. He did remember that I was a great Roundhead when I was a boy, and I was much afraid that he would have remembered the words that I said the day the King was beheaded (that, were I to preach upon him, my text should be—"The memory of the wicked shall rot"); but I found afterwards that he did go away from school before that time. He did make us good sport in imitating Mr. Case, Ash, and Nye, the ministers; which he did very well; but a deadly drinker he is, and grown exceeding fat.

# MR. PEPYS IS JEALOUS

APRIL 19TH, 1663 (Easter Day). After supper fell in discourse of dancing, and I find that Ashwell hath a very fine carriage, which makes my wife almost ashamed of herself to see herself so outdone; but to-morrow she begins to learn to dance for a month or two.

APRIL 25TH. Merrily practising to dance, which my wife hath begun to learn this day of Mr. Pembleton, but I fear will hardly do any good at it, because she is conceited that she do well already, though I think no such thing. So to bed.

MAY 4TH. The dancing-master came, instructing my wife; when he had done with her he would needs have me try the steps of a coranto; and what with his desire and my wife's importunity I did begin, and then was obliged to give him entry-money 10*s.*, and am become his scholler. The truth is I think it is a thing very useful for a gentleman, and sometimes I may have occasion of using it; and though it cost me what I am heartily sorry it should, besides that I must by my oath give half as much more to the poor, yet I am resolved to get it up some other way; and then it will not be above a month or two in a year. So though it be against my stomach, yet will I try it a little while; if I see it comes to any great inconvenience or charge I will fling it off. After I had begun with the steps of half a coranto, he went away.

MAY 12TH. Dined at noon at home, where a little angry with my wife for minding nothing now but the dancing-master, having him come twice a day, which is a folly.

MAY 13TH. At noon home to dinner, and after dinner Pembleton came and I practised. But, Lord! to see how my wife will not be thought to need telling by me or Ashwell, and yet will plead that she has learnt but a month, which causes many short fallings out between us. So to my office, whither one-eyed Cooper came to see me, and I made him to show me the use of platts, and to understand the lines, and how to find how lands bear, &c., to my great content.

MAY 15TH. Home, where I found it almost night, and my wife and the dancing-master alone above, not dancing but talking. Now so deadly full of jealousy I am that my heart and head did so cast about and fret that I could not do any business possibly, but went out to my office, and anon late home again and ready to chide at everything, and then suddenly to bed and could hardly sleep. But it is a deadly folly and plague that I bring upon myself to be so jealous and by giving myself such an occasion more than my wife desired of giving her another month's dancing. Which however shall be ended as soon as I can possibly. But I am ashamed to think what a course I did take by lying to see whether my wife did wear drawers to-day as she used to do, and other things to raise my suspicion of her, but I found no true cause of doing it.

MAY 16TH. Up with my mind disturbed and my last night's doubts upon me, for which I deserve to be beaten if not really

served as I am fearful of being; especially since God knows that I do not find honesty enough in my own mind but that upon a small temptation I could be false to her, and therefore ought not to expect more justice from her; but God pardon both my sin and my folly herein. To my office and there sitting all the morning, and at noon dined at home. After dinner comes Pembleton, and I being out of humour would not see him, pretending business. But Lord! with what jealousy did I walk up and down my chamber listening to hear whether they danced or no, which they did, notwithstanding I afterwards knew and did then believe that Ashwell was with them. So to my office awhile; and, my jealousy still reigning I went in and, not out of any pleasure but from that only reason, did go up to them to practise, and did make an end of "La Duchesse," which I think I should, with a little pains, do very well. So broke up and saw him gone. My mind in some better ease.

MAY 21ST. To dinner, my wife and I having high words about her dancing to that degree that I did enter and make a vow to myself not to oppose her or say anything to dispraise or correct her therein, as long as her month lasts, in pain of 2s. 6d. for every time, which, if God pleases, I will observe, for this roguish business has brought us more disquiett than anything [that] has happened a great while. After dinner to my office, where late, and then home; and Pembleton being there again we fell to dance a country dance or two, and so to supper and bed. But being at supper my wife did say something that caused me to oppose her in, she used the word devil, which vexed me, and among other things I said I would not have her to use that word, upon which she took me up most scornfully, which, before Ashwell and the rest of the world, I know not now-a-days how to check, as I would heretofore, for less than that would have made me strike her. So that I fear without great discretion I shall go near to lose too my command over her, and nothing do it more than giving her this occasion of dancing and other pleasures, whereby her mind is taken up from her business. But if this month of her dancing were but out (as my first was this night, and I paid off Pembleton for myself) I shall hope with a little pains to bring her to her old wont.

MAY 24TH (Lord's Day). At noon dined, and my wife telling me that there was a pretty lady come to Church with Peg Pen to-day, I against my intention had a mind to go to church to see her, and did so; and she is pretty handsome. But over against our gallery I espied Pembleton, and saw him leer upon my wife all the sermon, I taking no notice of him, and my wife upon him, and I observed she made a curtsey to him at coming out without taking notice to me at all of it, which with the consideration of her being desirous these two last Lord's days to go to church both forenoon and afternoon do really make me suspect something more than ordinary, though I am loth to think the worst; but yet it put and do still keep me at a great loss in my mind, and makes me curse the time that I consented to her dancing, and more my continuing it a second month, which was more than she desired, even after I had seen too much of her carriage with him. But I must have patience and get her into the country, or at least to make an end of her learning to dance as soon as I can.

MAY 26TH. Lay long in bed talking and pleasing myself with my wife. So up and to my office a while and then home, where I found Pembleton; and by many circumstances I am led to conclude that there is something more than ordinary between my wife and him, which do so trouble me that I know not at this very minute that I now write this almost what either I write or am doing, nor how to carry myself to my wife in it, being unwilling to speak of it to her for making of any breach and other inconveniences, nor let it pass for fear of her continuing to offend me and the matter grow worse thereby. So that I am grieved at the very heart; but I am very unwise in being so. There dined with me Mr. Creed and Captain Grove, and before dinner I had much discourse in my chamber with Mr. Deane about building of ships. But nothing could get the business out of my head, I fearing that this afternoon, by my wife's sending every [one] abroad and knowing that I must be at the office, she has appointed him to come. This is my devilish jealousy, which I pray God may be false, but it makes a very hell in my mind, which the God of heaven remove or I shall be very unhappy. So to the office, where we sat awhile. By and by my mind being in great trouble I went home to see how things were, and there I found as I doubted Mr. Pembleton with my wife, and nobody else in the house, which made me almost mad, and going up to my chamber after a turn or two I went out again and called somebody on pretence of business and left him in my little room at the door, telling him I would come again to him to speak with him about his business. So in great trouble and doubt to the office, and I made a quick end of our business and desired leave to be gone, pretending to go to the Temple, but it was home, and so up to my chamber. Continued in my chamber vexed and angry till he went away, pretending aloud, that I might hear, that he could not stay, and Mrs. Ashwell not being within they could not dance. And Lord! to see how my jealousy wrought so far that I went softly up to see whether any of the beds were out of order or no, which I found not, but that did not content me, but I staid all the evening walking, and though anon my wife came up to me, yet I construed it to be but impudence, and late put myself to bed in great discontent, and so to sleep.

MAY 27TH. So I waked by 3 o'clock, my mind being troubled, and so took occasion by making water to wake my wife, and after having lain till past 4 o'clock seemed going to rise, though I did it only to see what she would do, and so going out of the bed she took hold of me and would know what ailed me, and after many kind and some cross words I began to tax her discretion in yesterday's business, but she quickly told me my own, knowing well enough that it was my old disease of jealousy, which I denied, but to no purpose. After an hour's discourse, sometimes high and sometimes kind, I found very good reason to think that her freedom with him is very great and more than was convenient, but with no evil intent; and so after awhile I caressed her and parted seeming friends, but she crying in a great discontent. So I up and by water to the Temple. This day there was great thronging to Banstead Downs, upon a great horse-race and foot-race. I am sorry I could not go thither. So home back as I came, where I find my wife in a musty humour, and tells me before Ashwell that Pembleton had been there, and she would not have him come in unless I was there, which I was ashamed of, but however, I had rather it should be so than the other way. So to my office to put things in order there, and by and by comes Pembleton, and word is brought me from my wife thereof, that I might come home. So I sent word that I would have her go dance, and I would come presently. So being at a great loss whether I should appear to Pembleton or no, and what would most proclaim my jealousy to him, I at last resolved to go home; and my wife paid him off for this month also, and so he is cleared. After dancing we took him down to supper, and were very merry, and I made myself so, and kind to him as much as I could, to prevent his discourse, though I perceive to my trouble that he knows all, and may do me the disgrace to publish it as much as he can. Which I take very ill, and if too much provoked shall witness it to her. After supper and he gone we to bed.

JUNE 3RD. In the evening to the office and did some business, then home, and, God forgive me, did from my wife's unwillingness to tell me whither she had sent the boy, presently suspect that he was gone to Pembleton's, and from that occasion grew so discontented that I could hardly speak or sleep all night.

JUNE 4TH. Specially, I did by a wile get out of my boy that he did not yesterday go to Pembleton's or thereabouts, but only was sent all that time for some starch, and I did see him bringing home some, and yet all this cannot make my mind quiet.

AUGUST 16TH (Lord's Day). Up and with my wife to church, and finding her desirous to go to church, I did suspect her meeting of Pembleton, but he was not there, and so I thought my jealousy in vain, and treat the sermon with great quiet.

After dinner to church again, and there, looking up and down, I found Pembleton to stand in the aisle against us, he coming too late to get a pew. Which, Lord! into what a sweat did it put me!

## MRS. PEPYS IS JEALOUS

SEPTEMBER 24TH, 1667. This evening my wife tells me that W. Batelier hath been here to-day, and brought with him the pretty girl he speaks of, to come to serve my wife as a woman, out of the school at Bow. My wife says she is extraordinary handsome, and inclines to have her, and I am glad of it. But I shall leave it wholly to my wife.

SEPTEMBER 27TH. Up, and to the office, where very busy all the morning. While I was busy at the office, my wife sends for me to come home, and what was it but to see the pretty girl which she is taking to wait upon her: and though she seems not altogether so great a beauty as she had before told me, yet indeed she is mighty pretty; and so pretty that I find I shall be too much pleased with it, and therefore could be contented as to my judgment, though not to my passion, that she might not come, lest I may be found too much minding her, to the discontent of my wife. She is to come next week. She seems, by her discourse, to be grave beyond her bigness and age, and exceeding well bred as to her deportment, having been a scholar in a school at Bow these seven or eight years. To the office again, my head running on this pretty girl, and there till noon, when Creed and Sheres come and

35

dined with me; and we had a great deal of pretty discourse of the ceremoniousness of the Spaniards, whose ceremonies are so many and so known. My Lord Sandwich wears a beard now, turned up in the Spanish manner.

SEPTEMBER 30TH. So to Westminster, where to the Swan and drank, and away to the Hall, and thence to Mrs. Martin's to bespeak some linen, and there drank, and away. So by coach home, and there found our pretty girl Willet come, brought by Mr. Batelier, and she is very pretty, and so grave as I never saw a little thing in my life. Indeed I think her a little too good for my family, and so well carriaged as I hardly ever saw. I wish my wife may use her well.

DECEMBER 7TH. All the morning at the office, and at noon home to dinner with my clerks, and while we were at dinner comes Willet's aunt to see her and my wife; she is a very fine widow and pretty handsome but extraordinary well-carriaged and speaks very handsomely with extraordinary understanding, so as I spent the whole afternoon in her company with my wife, she understanding all the things of note touching plays and fashions and Court and everything and speaks rarely, which pleases me mightily, and seems to love her niece very well, and was so glad (which was pretty odde) that since she came hither her breasts began to swell, she being afeard before that she would have none, which was a pretty kind of content she gave herself.

DECEMBER 22ND (Lord's Day). Up, and then to dress myself and down to my chamber to settle some papers, and thither come to me Willet with an errand from her mistress, and this time I first did give her a little kiss, she being a very pretty humoured girle, and so one that I do love mightily. Thence to my office, and there did a little business, and so to church, where a dull sermon, and then home.

JANUARY 11TH, 1668. So up, and to the office, where all the morning busy, and thence home to dinner, and from dinner with Mercer, who dined with us, and wife and Deb. [Willet] to the King's house, there to see "The Wild Goose Chase," which I never saw, but have long longed to see it, being a famous play, but as it was yesterday I do find that where I expect most I do find least satisfaction, for in this play I met with nothing extraordinary at all, but very dull inventions and designs. Knepp come out and sat by us, and her talk pleased me a little, she telling me how Mis Davis is for certain going away from the Duke's house, the King being in love with her; and a house is taken for her, and furnishing; and she hath a ring given her already worth £600: that the King did send several times for Nelly* and she was with him, but what he did she knows not; this was a good while ago, and she says that the King first spoiled Mrs. Weaver, which is very mean, methinks, in a prince, and I am sorry for it, and can hope for no good to the state from having a Prince so devoted to his pleasure. And then home to supper, and so by the fireside to have my head combed, as I do now often do, by Deb., whom I love should be fiddling about me, and so to bed.

FEBRUARY 10TH. Home to my house to dinner, where I met Mr. Jackson, and find my wife angry with Deb., which vexes me.

---

*Nell Gwynn, perhaps the most famous and clever of Charles II's mistresses; an actress, as was Mrs. Knepp.

MARCH 31ST. Up pretty betimes and to the office, where we sat all the morning, and at noon I home to dinner, where also comes Mr. Hollier a little fuddled, and so did talk nothing but Latin, and laugh, that it was very good sport to see a sober man in such a humour, though he was not drunk to scandal. Mr. Pelling come and sat and talked late with us, and he being gone, I called Deb. to take pen, ink and paper and write down what things come into my head for my wife to do in order to her going into the country; and the girl, writing not so well as she would do, cried, and her mistress construed it to be sullenness, and so away angry with her too, but going to bed she undressed me, and there I did give her good advice and baiser la, elle* weeping still.

APRIL 2ND. Up, after much pleasant talk with my wife, and she got her ready to be gone, and by and by comes Betty Turner and her mother, and W. Batelier, and they and Deb., to whom I did give 10s. this morning, to oblige her to please her mistress (and ego did baiser her mouche †), and also Jane, and so in two coaches set out about eight o'clock towards the carrier, there for to take coach for my father's, that is to say, my wife and Betty Turner, Deb., and Jane; but I meeting my Lord Anglesey going to the Office, was forced to 'light in Cheapside, and there took my leave of them (not baisado Deb., which je ‡ had a great mind to), left them to go to their coach, and I to the office, where all the morning busy.

---

\* Pepys puts occasional words such as this into barbarously mangled and mingled foreign tongues. He is to be found mixing Latin, French, Spanish, Portuguese, Italian and English in one sentence. Here he means "kissed her, she weeping still."

† And I did kiss her mouth.

‡ Not kissing Deb., which I, etc.

# Samuel Pepys' Diary

*A short while later, being on a journey, Pepys and his family stop for a while in Deborah Willet's home village.*—EDITOR.

JUNE 13TH. So went to the Sun; and there Deb. going with W. Hewer and Betty Turner to see her uncle, and leaving my wife with the mistress of the house, I to see the Quay, which is a most large and noble place; and to see the new ship building. Walked back to the Sun, where I find Deb. come back, and with her, her uncle, a sober merchant, very good company, and so like one of our sober, wealthy, London merchants as pleased me mightily. Here we dined, and much good talk with him. Then walked with him and my wife and company round the quay, and to the ship; and he showed me the Custom-house, and made me understand many things of the place, and led us through Marsh Street, where our girl was born. But, Lord! the joy that was among the old poor people of the place, to see Mrs. Willet's daughter, it seems her mother being a brave woman and mightily beloved! And so brought us a back way by surprize to his house, where a substantial good house, and well furnished; and did give us good entertainment of strawberries, a whole venison-pasty cold, and plenty of brave wine, and above all Bristoll milk: where comes in another poor woman, who, hearing that Deb. was here, did come running hither, and with her eyes so full of tears, and heart so full of joy that she could not speak when she come in, that it made me weep too: I protest that I was not able to speak to her, which I would have done, to have diverted her tears. His wife a good woman, and so sober and substantiall as I was never more pleased anywhere. Servant-maid, 2s. So thence took leave, and he with us through the city, where in walking I find the city pay him great respect, and he the like to the meanest, which pleased me mightily. He shewed us the place where the merchants meet here, and a fine Cross yet standing, like Cheapside. We back, and by moonshine to the Bath again, about ten o'clock: bad way; and giving the coachman 1s., went all of us to bed.

AUGUST 10TH. So away to Cooper's, where I spent all the afternoon with my wife and girl, seeing him make an end of her picture, which he did to my great content: it is certainly a most rare piece of work, as to the painting. He hath £30 for his work, and the chrystal, and case, and gold case, comes to £8 3s. 4d.; and which I sent him this night, that I might be out of debt. And so by water home [to] supper, and my wife to read a ridiculous book I bought to-day of the History of the Taylor's Company; and all the while Deb. did comb my head.

OCTOBER 25TH (Lord's Day). Up, and discoursing with my wife about our house and many new things we are doing of, and so to church I. So home and to dinner, and after dinner all the afternoon got my wife and boy to read to me, and at night W. Batelier comes and sups with us; and after supper, to have my head combed by Deb., which occasioned the greatest sorrow to me that ever I knew in this world, for my wife, coming up suddenly, did find me embracing the girl. I was at a wonderful loss upon it, and the girle also, and I endeavored to put it off, but my wife was struck mute and grew angry, and so her voice come to her, grew quite out of order, and I to say little, but to bed, and my wife said little also, but could not sleep all night, but about two in the morning waked me and cried, and fell to tell me as a great secret that she was a Roman Catholique and had received the Holy Sacrament, which troubled me, but I took no notice of it, but she went on from one thing to another till at last it appeared plainly her trouble was at what she saw, but yet I did not know how much she saw, and therefore said nothing to her. But after her much crying and reproaching me with inconstancy and preferring a sorry girl before her, I did give her no provocation, but did promise all fair usage to her and love, and foreswore any hurt that I did with her, and so toward morning a little sleep, and so I with some little repose and rest.

OCTOBER 26TH. Rose, and up and by water to White Hall, but with my mind mightily troubled for the poore girle, whom I fear I have undone by this, my [wife] telling me that she would turn her out of doors. However, I was obliged to attend the Duke of York. Home and to dinner, finding my wife mightily discontented, and the girle sad, and no words from my wife to her. So after dinner they out with me about two or three things, and so home again, I all the evening busy, and my wife full of trouble in her looks, and anon to bed, where about midnight she wakes me, and there falls foul of me again, affirming that she saw me hug and kiss the girle; and upon her pressing me did offer to give her under my hand that I would never see Mrs. Pierce more, nor Knepp, but did promise her particular demonstrations of my true love to her, owning some indiscretions in what I did, but that there was no harm in it. She at last upon these promises was quiet, and very kind we were, and so to sleep.

OCTOBER 27TH. In the morning up, but my mind troubled for the poor girle, with whom I could not get opportunity to speak, but to the office, my mind mighty full of sorrow for her, where all the morning, and to dinner with my people, and to the office all afternoon, and so at night home, and there busy to get some things ready against to-morrow's meeting of Tangier, and that being done, and my clerks gone, my wife did towards bedtime begin to be in a mighty rage from some new matter that she had got in her head, and did most part of the night in bed rant at me in most high terms of threats of publishing my shame, and when I offered to rise would have rose too, and caused a candle to be light to burn by her all night in the chimney while she ranted, while the knowing myself to have given some grounds for it, did make it my business to appease her all I could possibly, and by good words and fair promises did make her very quiet, and so rested all night, and rose with perfect good peace, being heartily afflicted for this folly of mine that did occasion it, but was forced to be silent about the girle, which I have no mind to part with, but much less that the poor girle should be undone by my folly. So up with mighty kindness from my wife and a thorough peace, and being up did by a note advise the girle what I had done and owned, which note I was in pain for till she told me she had burned it. This evening Mr. Spong come, and first told me of the instrument called parallelogram,* which I must have one of, shewing me his practice thereon, by a map of England.

* A pantograph, used for reducing or increasing the scale of drawings. It operates on the principle of a double proportional compass.

NOVEMBER 3RD. Up, and all morning at the Office. At noon to dinner, and then to the Office, where busy till 12 at night, without much pain to my eyes, but I did not use them to read or write, and so did hold out very well. So home, and there to supper, and I observed my wife to eye my eyes whether I did ever look upon Deb., which I could not but do now and then (and to my grief did see the poor wretch look on me and see me look on her, and then let drop a tear or two, which do make my heart relent at this minute that I am writing this with great trouble of mind, for she is indeed my sacrifice, poor girle); and my wife did tell me in bed by the by of my looking on other people, and that the only way is to put things out of sight, and this I know she means by Deb., for she tells me that her aunt was here on Monday, and she did tell her of her desire of parting with Deb., but in such kind terms on both sides that my wife is mightily taken with her.

NOVEMBER 5TH. Up, and Willet come home in the morning, and, God forgive me! I could not conceal my content thereat by smiling, and my wife observed it, but I said nothing, nor she, but away to the Office.

NOVEMBER 6TH. Up, and presently my wife up with me, which she professedly now do every day to dress me, that I may not see Willet, and do eye me, whether I cast my eye upon her, or no, and do keep me from going into the room where she is among the upholsterers at work in our blue chamber.

NOVEMBER 8TH (Lord's Day). Up, and at my chamber all the morning, setting papers to rights, with my boy; and so to dinner at noon. The girle with us, but my wife troubled thereat to see her, and do tell me so, which troubles me, for I love the girle.

NOVEMBER 9TH. Up, and I did by a little note which I flung to Deb. advise her that I continue to deny that ever I kissed her, and so she might govern herself. The truth is that I did adventure upon God's pardoning me this lie, knowing how heavy a thing it would be for me to the ruin of the poor girle, and next knowing that if my wife should know all it were impossible ever for her to be at peace with me again, and so our whole lives would be uncomfortable. The girl read, and as I bid her returned me the note, flinging it to me in passing by. And so I abroad by [coach] to White Hall, and there to the Duke of York to wait on him.

NOVEMBER 10TH. Up, and my wife still every day as ill as she is all night, will rise to see me out of doors, telling me plainly that she dares not let me see the girle, and so I out to the office, where all the morning, and so home to dinner, where I found my wife mightily troubled again, more than ever, and she tells me that it is from her examining the girle, and getting a confession now from her of all. So my wife would not go down to dinner, but I would dine in her chamber with her, and there after mollifying her as much as I could we were pretty quiet and eat, and by and by we to talk again, and she to be troubled, reproaching me with my unkindness and perjury, I having denied my ever kissing her. As also with all her old kindnesses to me, and my ill-using of her from the beginning, and the many temptations she hath refused out of faithfulness to me, whereof several she was particular in, and especially from my Lord Sandwich, and then afterward the courtship of my Lord Hinchingbrooke, even to the trouble of his lady, all which I did acknowledge and was troubled for, and wept, and at last pretty good friends again, and so I to my office, and there late, and so home to supper with her, and so to bed, where, after half-an-hour's slumber she wakes me and cries out that she should never sleep more, and so kept raving till past midnight, that made me cry and weep heartily all the while for her, and troubled for what she reproached me with, as before, and at last with new vows, and particularly that I would myself bid the girle be gone, and shew my dislike to her, which I will endeavour to perform, but with much trouble, and so this appeasing her, we to sleep as well as we could till morning.

NOVEMBER 11TH. [To the Office], and there having done, I home and to supper and to bed, where, after lying a little while, my wife starts up, and with expressions of affright and madness, as one frantick, would rise, and I would not let her, but burst out in tears myself, and so continued almost half the night, the moon shining so that it was light, and after much sorrow and reproaches and little ravings (though I am apt to think they were counterfeit from her), and my promise again to discharge the girle myself, all was quiet again, and so to sleep.

NOVEMBER 12TH. Up, and she with me as heretofore, and so I to the Office, where all the morning, and at noon to dinner, and Mr. Wayth being at my office about business, I took him with me to talk and understand his matters, and so having dined we parted, and I to my wife and to sit with her a little, and then called her and Willet to my chamber, and there did, with tears in my eyes, which I could not help, discharge her and advise her to be gone as soon as she could, and never to see me, or let me see her more while she was in the house, which she took with tears too, but I believe understands me to be her friend, and I am apt to believe by what my wife hath of late told me is a cunning girle, if not a slut.

NOVEMBER 13TH. To White Hall, and there staid in Mr. Wren's chamber with him. Thence I home, and there to talk, with great pleasure all the evening, with my wife, who tells me that Deb. has been abroad to-day, and is come home and says she has got a place to go to, so as she will be gone to-morrow morning. This troubled me, and the truth is, I have a good mind to have the maidenhead of this girl. But she will be gone and I not know whither. Before we went to bed my wife told me she would not have me to see her or give her her wages, and so I did give my wife £10 for her year and half a quarter's wages, which she went into her chamber and paid her, and so to bed, and there, blessed be God! we did sleep well and with peace, which I had not done in now almost twenty nights together.

NOVEMBER 14TH. Up, but my wife would not let me out of her sight, and went down before me into the kitchen, and come up and told me that she [Deb.] was in the kitchen, and therefore would have me go round the other way; which she repeating and I vexed at it, answered her a little angrily, upon which she instantly flew out into a rage, calling me dog and rogue, and that I had a rotten heart; all which, knowing that I deserved it, I bore with, and word being brought presently up that she was gone away by coach with her things, my wife was friends, and so all quiet, and I to the Office, with my heart sad, and find that I cannot forget the girl, and vexed I know not where to look for her. And more troubled

to see how my wife is by this means likely for ever to have
her hand over me, that I shall for ever be a slave to her—
that is to say, only in matters of pleasure. Merry at noon, at
dinner; and after dinner to the Office, where all the afternoon, doing much business, late. My mind being free of all
troubles, I thank God, but only for my thoughts of this girl,
which hang after her.

NOVEMBER 15TH. My mind pretty quiet, and less troubled
about Deb. than I was, though yet I am troubled, I must confess, and would be glad to find her out, though I fear it would
be my ruin.

NOVEMBER 16TH. Up, and by water to White Hall. This
being done I away to Holborne, about Whetstone's Park,
where I never was in my life before, where I understand by
my wife's discourse that Deb. is gone, which do trouble me
mightily that the poore girle should be in desperate condition
forced to go thereabouts, and there not hearing of any such
man as Allbon, with whom my wife had said she now was,
I find that this Dr. Allbon is a kind of poor broken fellow
that dare not shew his head, nor be known where he is gone.

NOVEMBER 17TH. At my office all the afternoon and at night
busy, and so home to my wife, and pretty pleasant, and at
mighty ease in my mind, being in hopes to find Deb., and
without trouble or the knowledge of my wife. So home to
supper at night and to bed.

NOVEMBER 18TH. Lay long in bed talking with my wife, she
being unwilling to have me go abroad, saying and declaring
herself jealous of my going out for fear of my going to Deb.,
which I do deny, for which God forgive me, for I was no
sooner out about noon but I did go by coach directly to

Somerset House, and there enquired among the porters there for Dr. Allbun, and the first I spoke with told me he knew him, and that he was newly gone into Lincoln's Inn Fields, but whither he could not tell me, but that one of his fellows not then in the way did carry a chest of drawers thither with him, and that when he comes he would ask him. This put me into some hopes, and towards night did meet with the porter that carried the chest of drawers with this Doctor, but he would not tell me where he lived, being his good master, he told me, but if I would have a message to him he would deliver it. At last I told him my business was not with him, but with a little gentlewoman, one Mrs. Willet, that is with him, and sent him to see how she did from her friend in London, and no other token. He goes while I walk in Somerset House, walked there in the Court; at last he comes back and tells me she is well, and that I may see her if I will, but no more. So I could not be commanded by my reason, but I must go this very night, and so by coach, it being now dark, I to her, close by my tailor's, and she come into the coach to me, and je* did baiser her. I did nevertheless give her the best council I could, to have a care of her honour, and to fear God, and suffer no man para avoir to do con her as je have done, which she promised. Je did give her 20s. and directions para laisser sealed in paper at any time the name of the place of her being at Herringman's, my bookseller in the 'Change, by which I might go para her, and so bid her good night with much content to my mind, and resolution to look after her no more till I heard from her. And so home, and there told

* *Je*, I; *baiser*, kiss; *para avoir*, to have; *con*, with; *para laisser*, how to leave; *para*, to.

my wife a fair tale, God knows, how I spent the whole day, with which the poor wretch was satisfied, or at least seemed so, and so to supper and to bed, she having been mighty busy all day in getting of her house in order against to-morrow to hang up our new hangings and furnishing our best chamber.

NOVEMBER 19TH. Up, and at the Office all the morning, with my heart full of joy to think in what a safe condition all my matters now stand between my wife and Deb. and me, and at noon running up stairs to see the upholsterers, who are at work upon hanging my best room, and setting up my new bed, I find my wife sitting sad in the dining room; which enquiring into the reason of, she began to call me all the false, rotten-hearted rogues in the world, letting me understand that I was with Deb. yesterday, which, thinking it impossible for her ever to understand, I did awhile deny, but at last did, for the ease of my mind and hers, and forever to discharge my heart of this wicked business, I did confess all: and above stairs in our bed-chamber there I did endure the sorrow of her threats and vows and curses all the afternoon, and, what was worse, she swore by all that was good that she would slit the nose of this girle, and be gone herself this very night from me, and did there demand 3 or £400 of me to buy my peace, that she might be gone without making any noise, or else protested that she would make all the world know of it. So with most perfect confusion of face and heart, and sorrow and shame, in the greatest agony in the world I did pass this afternoon, fearing that it will never have an end; but at last I did call for W. Hewer, who I was forced to make privy now to all, and the poor fellow did cry like a child, [and] obtained what I could not, that she would be pacified upon condition that I would give it under my hand never to see or speak with Deb. while I live, as I did before with Pierce and Knepp, and which I did also, God knows, promise for Deb. too, but I have the confidence to deny it to the perjury of myself. So, before it was late, there was, beyond my hopes as well as desert, a durable peace; and so to supper, and pretty kind words, and to bed, and so with some rest spent the night.

NOVEMBER 20TH. This morning up, with mighty kind words between my poor wife and I; and so to White Hall by water, W. Hewer with me, who is to go with me every where, until my wife be in condition to go out along with me herself; for she do plainly declare that she dares not trust me out alone, and therefore made it a piece of our league that I should always take somebody with me, or her herself, which I am mighty willing to, being by the grace of God, resolved never to do her wrong more. We landed at the Temple, and there I bid him call at my cozen Roger Pepys's lodgings, and I staid in the street for him, and so took water again at the Strand stairs; and so to White Hall, in my way I telling him plainly and truly my resolutions, if I can get over this evil, never to give new occasion for it. He is, I think, so honest and true a servant to us both, and one that loves us, that I was not much troubled at his being privy to all this, but rejoiced in my heart that I had him to assist in the making of us friends, which he did truly and heartily, and with good success, for I did get him to go to Deb. to tell her that I had told my wife all of my being with her the other night, that so if my wife should send she might not make the business worse by denying it. While I was at White Hall with the Duke of York, doing our ordinary business with him, W. Hewer did go to her and come back again, and so I took him into St. James's Park, and there he did tell me he had been with her, and found what I said about my manner of being with her true, and had given her advice as I desired. I did there enter into more talk about my wife and myself, and he did give me great assurance of several particular cases to which my wife had from time to time made him privy of her loyalty and truth to me after many and great temptations, and I believe them truly. I did this night promise to my wife never to go to bed without calling upon God upon my knees by prayer, and I begun this night, and hope I shall never forget to do the like all my life; for I do find that it is much the best for my soul and body.

NOVEMBER 23RD. I met with Mr. Povy, who I discoursed with about publick business. Thence with W. Hewer, who goes up and down with me like a jaylour, but yet with great love, and to my great good liking.

NOVEMBER 25TH. My wife and I to the Duke of York's house, to see "The Duchesse of Malfy," a sorry play, and sat with little pleasure, for fear of my wife's seeing me look about, and so I was uneasy all the while, though I desire and resolve never to give her trouble of that kind more. So home at noon to dinner, where I find Mr. Pierce and his wife, but I was forced to shew very little pleasure in her being there because of my vow to my wife.

NOVEMBER 29TH (Lord's Day). Lay long in bed with pleasure [with my wife], and my mind is mightily more at ease, and I do mind my business better than ever and am more at peace, and trust in God I shall ever be so, though I cannot yet get my mind off from thinking now and then of Deb.;

but I do ever since my promise a while since to my wife pray to God by myself in my chamber every night, and will endeavour to get my wife to do the like with me ere long.

NOVEMBER 30TH. Up betimes, and with W. Hewer, who is my guard, to White Hall, to a Committee of Tangier.

DECEMBER 18TH. I have a new fight with my wife, who is under new trouble by some news she hath heard of Deb.'s being mighty fine, and gives out that she has a friend that gives her money, and this my wife believes to be me, and, poor wretch! I cannot blame her, and therefore she run into mighty extremes.

JANUARY 5TH, 1669. Up, and after a little talk with my wife, which troubled me, she being ever since our late difference mighty watchful of sleep and dreams, and will not be persuaded but I do dream of Deb., and do tell me that I speak in my dreams and that this night I did cry, Huzzy, and it must be she, and now and then I start otherwise than I used to do, she says, which I know not, for I do not know that I dream of her more than usual, though I cannot deny that my thoughts waking do run now and then against my will and judgment upon her, for that only is wanting to undo me, being now in every other thing as to my mind most happy, and may still be so but for my own fault, if I be catched loving any body but my wife again.

JANUARY 7TH. This afternoon, passing through Queen's Street, I saw pass by our coach on foot Deb., which, God forgive me, did put me into some new thoughts of her, and for her, but durst not shew them, and I think my wife did not see her, but I did get my thoughts free of her as soon as I could.

# Samuel Pepys' Diary

JANUARY 12TH. This evening I observed my wife mighty dull, and I myself was not mighty fond, because of some hard words she did give me at noon, out of a jealousy at my being abroad this morning, which, God knows, it was upon the business of the Office unexpectedly; but I to bed, not thinking but she would come after me. But waking by and by out of a slumber, which I usually fall into presently after my coming into the bed, I found she did not prepare to come to bed, but got fresh candles, and more wood for her fire, it being mighty cold, too. At this being troubled, I after a while prayed her to come to bed, all my people being gone to bed; so, after an hour or two, she silent, and I now and then praying her to come to bed, she fell out into a fury, that I was a rogue, and false to her. But yet I did perceive that she was to seek what to say, only she invented, I believe, a business that I was seen in a hackney coach with the glasses up with Deb., but could not tell the time, nor was sure I was he. I did, as I might truly, deny it, and was mightily troubled, but all would not serve. At last about one o'clock she came to my side of the bed and drew the curtaine open, and with the tongs red hot at the ends, at which in dismay I rose up, and with a few words she laid them down, and did by little and little, and very sillily, let all the discourse fall; and about two, but with much seeming difficulty, come to bed, and there lay well all night, and long in bed talking together with much pleasure, it being, I know, nothing but her doubt of my going out yesterday without telling her of my going, which did vex her, poor wretch! last night, and I cannot blame her jealousy, though it do vex me to the heart.

MARCH 12TH. In my coach with W. Hewer towards West-minster; and there to Nott's, the famous bookbinder, that bound for my Lord Chancellor's library; and here I did take occasion for curiosity to bespeak a book to be bound, only that I might have one of his binding. And so home, where, thinking to meet my wife with content, after my pains all this day, I find her in a closet, alone, in the dark, in a hot fit of railing against me, upon some news she has heard of Deb.'s living very fine, and with black spots, and speaking ill words of her mistress, which with good reason might vex her; and the baggage is to blame, but, God knows, I know nothing of her, nor what she do, nor what becomes of her, though God knows that my devil that is within me do wish that I could. But in her fit she did tell me what vexed me all the night, that this had put her upon putting off her handsome maid and hiring another that was full of the small pox, which did mightily vex me, though I said nothing, and do still.

APRIL 13TH. Sent for W. Hewer, and he and I by water to White Hall to look, among other things, for Mr. May, to unbespeak his dining with me tomorrow. But here being in the court-yard, as God would have it, I spied Deb., which made my heart and head to work, and I presently could not refrain, but sent W. Hewer away to look for Mr. Wren (W. Hewer, I perceive, did see her, but whether he did see me see her or not, or suspect my sending him away I know not, but my heart could not hinder me), and I run after her and two women and a man, more ordinary people, and she in her old clothes; and after hunting a little, find them in the lobby of the chapel below stairs, and there I observed she endeavoured to avoid me, but I did speak to her and she to me, and did get her pour dire* me ou she demeurs now, and did charge her para say nothing of me that I had vu elle, which she did promise, and so with my heart full of surprize and disorder I away, and meeting with Sir H. Cholmley walked into the Park with him and back again, looking to see if I could spy her again in the Park, but I could not. And so home to my wife, who is come home from Deptford. But, God forgive me, I hardly know how to put on confidence enough to speak as innocent, having had this passage to-day with Deb., though only, God knows, by accident. But my great pain is lest God Almighty shall suffer me to find out this girl, whom indeed I love, and with a bad amour; but I will pray to God to give me grace to forbear it. So home to supper, where very sparing in my discourse, not giving occasion of any enquiry where I have been to-day, or what I have done, and so without any trouble to-night more than my fear, we to bed.

APRIL 14TH. Up and with W. Hewer to White Hall, and there I did speak with the Duke of York, the Council sitting in the morning. Thence home, and there to talk and to supper and to bed, all being very safe as to my seeing of poor Deb. yesterday.

APRIL 15TH. Up, and to the office, and thence before the office sat to the Excise Office with W. Hewer, but found some occasion to go another way to the Temple on business, and I by Deb.'s direction did know whither in Jewen Street to direct my hackney coachman. Thence I away, and through Jewen Street, my mind, God knows, running that way, but stopped not, but going down Holborne Hill, by the Conduit, I did see Deb., on foot going up the hill. I saw her, and she

* *Pour dire,* to say; *ou,* where; *demeurs,* lives; *vu elle,* seen her.

me, but she made no stop, but seemed unwilling to speak to me; so I a way on, and then stopped and 'light, and after her and overtook her at the end of Hosier lane in Smithfield, and without standing in the street desired her to follow me, and I led her into a little blind alehouse within the walls, and there she and I alone fell to talk and baiser la * and toker su mamailles, but she mighty coy, and I hope modest. I did give her in a paper 20s., and we did agree para meet again in the hall at Westminster on Monday next; and so giving me great hopes by her carriage that she continues modest and honest, we did there part, she going home and I to Mrs. Turner's.

APRIL 19TH. Up, and with Tom by coach to White Hall, and there having set him work in the Robe Chamber, to write something for me, I to Westminster Hall and there walked from 10 o'clock to past 12, expecting to have met Deb., but whether she had been there before, and missing me went away, or is prevented in coming, I know not; but she not then appearing, I being tired with walking, went home.

APRIL 26TH. Myself and wife went down the Temple, and just at the Temple gate I spied Deb., with another gentle-woman, and Deb. winked on me and smiled, but undiscovered, and I was glad to see her.

MAY 7TH. With my wife abroad, with our coach, most pleasant weather; and to Hackney, and into the marshes, where I never was before, and thence round about to Old Ford and Bow; and coming through the latter home, there being some young gentle-women at a door, and I seeming not to know who they were, my wife's jealousy told me presently that I knew well enough it was that damned place where Deb.

---

* Baiser la, kiss her; toker su mamailles, play with her breasts; para, to.

dwelt, which made me swear very angrily that it was false, as it was. So I continued out of humour for a good while at it, she being willing to be friends, so I was by and by, saying no more of it.

MAY 31ST. My amours to Deb. are past.

*Which last is the final word of the diary in respect to Deb., poor girl.*—EDITOR.

## STAGES OF AFFLUENCE, AND SOME SOURCES

INTRODUCTORY REMARKS, JANUARY 1ST, 1660. My own private condition very handsome, and esteemed rich, but indeed very poor; besides my goods of my house, and my office, which at present is somewhat uncertain.

JANUARY 29TH. Went home and spent the afternoon in casting up my accounts, and do find myself to be worth £40 or more, which I did not think, but am afraid that I have forgot something.

MAY 26TH. This night the Captain told me that my Lord hath appointed me £30 out of the 1000 ducats which the King had given to the ship, at which my heart was very much joyed.

JUNE 3RD. At sermon in the morning; after dinner into my cabin, to cast my accounts up, and find myself to be worth near £100, for which I bless Almighty God, it being more than I hoped for so soon, being I believe not clearly worth £25 when I came to sea. Then to set my papers in order, they being increased much upon my hands.

JULY 7TH. To my Lord, one with me to buy a Clerk's place, and I did demand £100. To the Council Chamber, where I took an order for the advance of the salaries of the officers of the Navy, and I find mine to be raised to £350 * per annum. Thence to the Change, where I bought two fine prints from Rubens, and afterwards dined.

July 27th. The last night Sir W. Batten and Sir W. Pen came to their houses at the office. Met this morning and did business till noon. Will, my clerk and I were all the afternoon making up my accounts, which we had done by night, and I find myself worth about £100 after all my expenses.

August 2nd. Dined with Mr. Blackburne at his house with his friends, where we were very well treated and merry. From thence W. Hewer and I to the office of Privy Seal, where I stayed all afternoon, and received about £40 for yesterday and to-day, at which my heart rejoiced for God's blessing to me, to give me this advantage by chance, there being of this £40 about £10 due to me for this day's work. So great is the present profit of this office, above what it was in the King's time; there being the last month about 300 bills, whereas in the late King's time it was much to have 40. With my money home by coach, it being the first time that I could get home before our gates were shut since I came to the Navy office.

August 10th. After dinner with great pain in my back I went by water to Whitehall to the Privy Seal. Blessed be God for my good chance of the Privy Seal, where I get every day I believe about £3. This place I got by chance, and my Lord did give it me by chance, neither he nor I thinking it to be of the worth that he and I find it to be. Never since I was a man in the world was I ever so great a stranger to public affairs as now I am, having not read a new book or anything

---

* Pepys was constrained to divide this with one Barlow, who had preceded him in the position. See the entry under February 9th, 1665.

like it, or enquiring after any news, or what the Parliament do, or in any wise how things go. Many people look after my house in Axe-yard to hire it.

AUGUST 16TH. This morning my Lord (all things being ready) carried me by coach to Mr. Crew's, (in the way talking how good he did hope my place would be to me, and in general speaking that it was not the salary of any place that did make a man rich, but the opportunity of getting money while he is in the place) where he took leave, and went into the coach, and so for Hinchinbroke.

SEPTEMBER 5TH. To the office, home to dinner, where (having put away my boy in the morning) his father brought him again, but I did so clear up my boy's roguery to his father, that he could not speak against my putting him away, and so I did give him 10s. and tore his indenture. In the evening, my wife being a little impatient, I went along with her to buy a necklace of pearl, which will cost £4 10s., which I am willing to comply with her in for her encouragement, and because I have lately got money, having now above £200 in cash beforehand in the world. Home, and having in our way bought a rabbit and two little lobsters, my wife and I did sup late, and so to bed.

OCTOBER 31ST. This month I conclude with my mind very heavy for the greatness of my late expenses, insomuch that I do not think that I have above £150 clear money in the world, but I have, I believe, got a great deal of good household stuff. My wife has been so ill of late, of her old pain, that I have not known her this fortnight almost, which is a pain to me.

DECEMBER 10TH. Into my study, and to ease my mind did go to cast up how my cash stands, and I do find as near as I can that I am worth in money clear £240, for which God be praised.

DECEMBER 12TH. Up with J. Spicer to his office and took £100, and by coach with it as far as my father's, where I called to see them, and my father did offer me six pieces of gold, in lieu of £6 that he borrowed of me the other day, but it went against me to take it of him and therefore did not, though I was afterwards a little troubled that I did not. Thence home, and took out this £100 and sealed it up with the other last night, it being the first £200 that ever I saw together of my own in my life. After that home and to bed, reading myself asleep, while the wench sat mending my breeches by my bedside.

DECEMBER 31ST. I take myself now to be worth £300 clear in money, and all my goods and all manner of debts paid, which are none at all.

FEBRUARY 15TH, 1661. At the office all the morning, and in the afternoon at making up my accounts for my Lord to-morrow; and that being done I found myself to be clear (as I think) £350 in the world, besides my goods in my house and all things paid for.

MAY 24TH. At home all the morning making up my private accounts, and this is the first time that I do find myself to be clearly worth £500 in money, besides all my goods in my house, &c. In the afternoon at the office late, and then I went to the Wardrobe, where I found my Lord at supper, and therefore I walked a good while till he had done, and I went in to him, and there he looked over my accounts, and they were committed to Mr. Moore. Then down to the kitchen to eat a bit of bread and butter, which I did, and there I took one of the maids by the chin. From thence home.

JUNE 30TH (Lord's Day). To church, and then home to dinner, my wife and I all alone. I to Graye's Inn Walk, all alone, and with great pleasure seeing the fine ladies walk there. Myself humming to myself (which now-a-days is my constant practice since I begun to learn to sing) the trillo, and found by use that it do come upon me. Myself lately upon a great expense of money upon myself in clothes and other things, but I hope to make it up this summer by my having to do in getting things ready to send with the next fleet to the Queen. Myself in good health, but mighty apt to take cold, so that this hot weather I am fain to wear a cloth before my belly.

DECEMBER 31ST. I suppose myself to be worth about £500 clear in the world, and my goods of my house my own, and what is coming to me from Brampton when my father dies, which God defer.

MARCH 1ST, 1662. I settled to what I had long intended, to cast up my accounts with myself, and after much pains to do it and great fear, I do find that I am £500 in money beforehand in the world, which I was afraid I was not; but I find I had spent above £250 this last half year, which troubles me much, but by God's blessing I am resolved to take up.

MAY 30TH. This morning I made up my accounts, and find myself de claro worth about £530, and no more, so little have I increased it since my last reckoning; but I confess I have laid out much money in clothes.

JULY 31ST. It being the last day of the month, I did make up my accounts before I went to bed, and found myself worth about £650, for which the Lord God be praised, and so to bed.

I drank but two glasses of wine this day, and yet it makes my head ake all night, and indisposed me all the next day, of which I am glad. I am now in town only with my man Will and Jane.

AUGUST 31ST (Lord's Day). So to my office, and there made my monthly accounts, and I find myself worth in money about £686 19s. 2½d., for which God be praised; and indeed greatly I hope to thank Almighty God, who do most manifestly bless me in my endeavours to do the duties of my office, I now saving money, and my expenses very little.

SEPTEMBER 30TH. I made up this evening my monthly ballance, and find that, notwithstanding the loss of £30 to be paid to the loyall and necessitous cavaliers by act of Parliament, yet I am worth about £680, for which the Lord God be praised.

DECEMBER 31ST. Thus ends this year with great mirth to me and my wife. Our condition being thus: we are at present spending a night or two at my Lord's lodgings at White Hall. Our home at the Navy-office, which is and hath a pretty while been in good condition, finished and made very convenient. My purse is worth about £650, besides my goods of all sorts, which yet might have been more but for my late layings out upon my house and public assessment, and yet would not have been so much if I had not lived a very orderly life all this year by virtue of the oaths that God put into my heart to take against wine, plays and other expenses, and to observe for these last twelve months and which I am now going to renew, I under God owing my present content thereunto.

APRIL 3RD, 1663. I met Captain Grove, who did give me a letter directed to myself from himself. I discerned money to be in it, and took it, knowing, as I found it to be, the proceed of the place I have got him to be, the taking up of vessels for Tangier. But I did not open it till I came home to my office, and there I broke it open, not looking into it till all the money was out, that I might say I saw no money in the paper, if ever I should be questioned about it. There was a piece in gold and £4 in silver. So home to dinner with my father and wife, and after dinner up to my tryangle, where I found that above my expectation Ashwell has very good principles of musique and can take out a lesson herself with very little pains, at which I am very glad.

JUNE 30TH. Some money I do and can lay up, but not much, being worth now above £700, besides goods of all sorts.

JULY 31ST. Up early to my accounts this month, and I find myself worth clear £730, the most I ever had yet, which contents me though I encrease but very little. Thence to my office doing business, and at noon to my viall maker's and so to the Exchange, where I met Dr. Pierce. He tells me, as a friend, the great injury that he thinks I do myself by being so severe in the Yards. Now I discharge a good conscience therein, and I tell him that no man can (nor do he say any say it) charge me with doing wrong.

SEPTEMBER 30TH. To my office, and there I sat late making up my month's accounts, and, blessed be God do find myself £760 creditor, notwithstanding that for clothes for myself and wife, I have spent this month £47.

OCTOBER 31ST. To the office, where busy till night, and then to prepare my monthly account, about which I staid till 10 or 11 o'clock at night, and to my great sorrow find myself £43 worse than I was the last month, which was then £760, and

now it is but £717. I hope I shall not need now to lay out more money a great while.

DECEMBER 10TH. To my book-seller's, and having gained this day in the office by my stationer's bill to the King about 40s. or £3, I did here sit two or three hours calling for twenty books to lay this money out upon, and found myself at a great losse where to choose, and do see how my nature would gladly return to laying out money in this trade.

DECEMBER 12TH. To the Exchange, where I had sent Luellin word I would come to him, and thence brought him home to dinner with me. Then he began to tell me that Mr. Deering had been with him to desire to speak to me that if I would get him off with these goods upon his hands, he would give me 50 pieces, and further that if I would stand his friend to help him to the benefit of his patent as the King's merchant he could spare me £200 per annum out of his profits. I was glad to hear both of these, but answered him no further than that as I would not by anything be bribed to be unjust in my dealings, so I was not so squeamish as not to take people's acknowledgement where I had the good fortune by my pains to do them good and just offices, and so I would not come to be at any agreement with him, but I would labor to do him this service and to accept his consideration thereof afterward as he thought fit. So I expect to hear more of it. I did make very much of Luellin in hopes to have some good by this business. I spent a little time walking in the garden, and in the mean time, while I was walking, Mrs. Pen's pretty maid came by my side, and went into the office, but finding nobody there I went in to her, being glad of the occasion.

DECEMBER 29TH. After dinner Luellin took me up to my chamber to give me £50 for the service I did him, though not so great as he expected and I intended. But I told him I would not sell my liberty to any man. I did also tell him that neither this nor any thing should make me do any thing that should not be for the King's service besides.

DECEMBER 31ST. In my chamber sat till 4 o'clock in the morning making up my accounts and writing this last Journall of the year. And first I bless God I do, after a large expense, find that I am worth in money above £800, whereof in my Lord Sandwich's hand £700, and the rest in my hand. For which the good God be pleased to give me a thankful heart and a mind careful to preserve this and increase it.

FEBRUARY 2ND, 1664. Off to the Sun Taverne with Sir W. Warren, and among other things he did give me a payre of gloves for my wife wrapt up in paper, which I would not open, feeling it hard; but did tell him that my wife should thank him, and so went on in discourse. When I came home, Lord! in what pain I was to get my wife out of the room without bidding her go, that I might see what these gloves were; and by and by, she being gone, it proves a payre of white gloves for her and forty pieces in good gold, which did so cheer my heart that I could eat no victuals almost for dinner for joy to think how God do bless us every day more and more, and more yet I hope he will upon the increase of my duty and endeavours. I was at great losse what to do, whether tell my wife of it or no, which I could hardly forbear, but yet I did and will think of it first before I do, for fear of making her think me to be in a better condition, or in a better way of getting money, than yet I am.

MAY 2ND. We home, and to my office, whither comes Mr.
Bland, and pays me the debt he acknowledged he owed me for
my service in his business of the Tangier Merchant, twenty
pieces of new gold, a pleasant sight. It cheered my heart; and
he being gone, I home to supper, and shewed them to my
wife; and she, poor wretch, would fain have kept them to
look on, without any other design but a simple love to them,
but I thought it not convenient, and so took them into my
own hand. So, after supper, to bed.

JULY 18TH. To Westminster to my barber's, to have my Peri-
wigg he lately made me cleansed of its nits, which vexed me
cruelly that he should put such a thing into my hands. Here
meeting his mayde Jane, that has lived with them so long, I
talked with her, and sending her of an errand to Dr. Clerk's,
did meet her, and took her into a little alehouse in Brewer's
Yard, and there did sport with her, without any knowledge of
her though, and a very pretty innocent girl she is. Thence
home and Creed with me, and there he took occasion to owne
his obligations to me, and did lay down twenty pieces in gold
upon my shelf in my closett, which I did not refuse, but wish
and expected should have been more. But, however, this is
better than nothing, and now I am out of expectation, and
shall henceforward know how to deal with him.

JULY 21ST. This morning to the office comes Nicholas
Osborne, Mr. Gauden's clerk, to desire of me what piece of
plate I would choose to have a £100 or thereabouts, bestowed
on me. I a great while urged my unwillingness to take any,
not knowing how I could serve Mr. Gauden, but left it wholly
to himself; so at noon I find brought home in fine leather
cases a pair of the noblest flaggons that ever I saw all the days

of my life; whether I shall keep them or no I cannot tell, for it is to oblige me to him in the business of the Tangier victualling, wherein I doubt I shall not; but glad I am to see that I shall be sure to get something on one side or other, have it which will: so, with a merry heart, I looked upon them, and locked them up.

JULY 31ST (Lord's Day). Up, and to church, where I have not been these many weeks. Mr. Hill and I to my house, and there to musique all the afternoon. He being gone, in the evening I to my accounts, and to my great joy and with great thanks to Almighty God, I do find myself most clearly worth £1,014, the first time that ever I was worth £1,000 before, which is the height of all that ever I have for a long time pretended to. But by the blessing of God upon my care I hope to lay up something more in a little time, if this business of the victualling of Tangier goes on as I hope it will. So with praise to God for this state of fortune that I am brought to as to wealth, I home to supper and to bed, desiring God to give me the grace to make good use of what I have, and continue my care and diligence to gain more.

AUGUST 7TH (Lord's Day). Lay long caressing my wife and talking. So up and ready, and my wife also, and then down, and I showed my wife, to her great admiration and joy, Mr. Gauden's present of plate, the two flaggons, which indeed are so noble that I hardly can think they are yet mine. So blessing God for it, we down to dinner mighty pleasant, and so up after dinner for a while, and I then to White Hall, walked thither.

SEPTEMBER 30TH. Up, and all day, both morning and afternoon, at my accounts, it being a great month, both for profit and laying out, the last being £89 for kitchen and clothes for myself and wife, and a few extraordinaries for the house; and my profits, besides salary, £239; so that I have this weeke my balance to come to £1,203, for which the Lord's name be praised!

DECEMBER 31ST. At the office all the morning, and after dinner there again, dispatched first my letters, and then to my accounts, not of the month but of the whole year also, and was at it till past twelve at night, it being bitter cold; but yet I was well satisfied with my worke, and, above all, to find myself, by the great blessing of God, worth £1,349, by which, as I have spent very largely, so I have laid up above £500 this yeare above what I was worth this day twelvemonth. The Lord make me forever thankful to his holy name for it! Thence home to eat a little and so to bed. Soon as ever the clock struck one, I kissed my wife in the kitchen by the fireside, wishing her a merry new yeare, observing that I believe I was the first proper wisher of it this year, for I did it as soon as ever the clock struck one.

FEBRUARY 9TH, 1665. Sir William Petty come, among other things, to tell me that Mr. Barlow is dead; for which, God knows my heart, I could be as sorry as is possible for one to be for a stranger, by whose death he gets £100 per annum, he being a worthy, honest man; but after having considered that when I come to consider the providence of God by this means unexpectedly to give me £100 a year more in my estate, I have cause to bless God, and do it from the bottom of my heart. So home late at night, after twelve o'clock, and so to bed.

FEBRUARY 28TH. Come home, I to the taking of my wife's kitchen accounts at the latter end of this month, and there find 7s. wanting, which did occasion a very high falling out between us, I indeed too angrily insisting upon so poor a thing, and did give her very provoking high words, calling her beggar, and reproaching her friends, which she took very stomachfully and reproached me justly with mine, and I confess, being myself, I cannot see what she could have done less. We parted after many high words very angry, and I to my office to my month's accounts, and find myself worth £1,270, for which the Lord God be praised.

MARCH 16TH. This afternoon Mr. Harris, the sayle-maker, sent me a noble present of two large silver candle-sticks and snuffers, and a slice to keep them upon, which indeed is very handsome. At night come Mr. Andrews with £36, the further fruits of my Tangier contract, and so to bed late and weary with business, but in good content of mind, blessing God for these his benefits.

MARCH 17TH. To the Committee of Tangier, where the Duke a little, and then left us. The whole business was the stating of Povy's accounts, of whom to say no more, never could man say worse himself nor have worse said of him than was by the company to his face; I mean, as to his folly and very reflecting words to his honesty. Broke up without anything but trouble and the most open shame to him and high words to him of disgrace that they would not trust him with any more money till he had given an account of this. So broke up. Then he took occasion to desire me to step aside, and he and I by water to London together. In the way, of his owne accord, he proposed to me that he would surrender his place of Treasurer to me to have half the profit. The thing is new to me; but the more I think the more I like it, and do put him upon getting it done by the Duke. Whether it takes or no I care not, but I think at present it may have some convenience in it.

MARCH 18TH. Povy and Creed and I to do some business upon Povy's accounts all the afternoon till late at night, where, God help him! never man was so confounded, and all his people about him in this world as he and his are. After we had done something [to the] purpose we broke up, and Povy acquainted me before Creed (having said something of it also this morning at our office to me) what he had done in speaking to the Duke and others about his making me Treasurer, and has carried it a great way, so as I think it cannot well be set back.

MARCH 19TH (Lord's Day). To my Lord Sandwich's to dinner, and after dinner to Mr. Povy's, who hath been with the Duke of Yorke, and, by the mediation of Mr. Coventry, the Duke told him that the business shall go on, and he will take off Brunkerd. Being very glad of this news, Mr. Povy and I in his coach to Hyde Park. Where many brave ladies; among others, Castlemayne lay impudently upon her back in her coach asleep, with her mouth open.

MARCH 20TH. To St. James's, and there was in great doubt of Brunkerd. The Duke did direct Secretary Bennet to declare his mind to the Tangier Committee, that he approves of me for Treasurer: and with a character of me to be a man whose industry and discretion he would trust soon as any man's in England: and did the like to my Lord Sandwich.

APRIL 30TH (Lord's Day). I with great joy find myself to have gained this month above £100 clear, and in the whole to be worth above £1,400, the greatest sum I ever yet was worth. Thus I end this month in great content as to my estate and gettings: in much trouble as to the pains I have taken, and the rubs I expect to meet with, about the business of Tangier.

AUGUST 2ND. Up, it being a publique fast, as being the first Wednesday of the month, for the plague. I within doors all day, and upon my monthly accounts late, I did find myself really worth £1,900, for which the great God of Heaven and Earth be praised!

AUGUST 14TH. By water to Woolwich where supped with my wife and then to bed betimes. This night I did present my wife with the dyamond ring, awhile since given me by Mr. Dicke Vines's brother, for helping him to be a purser, valued at about £10, the first thing of that nature I did ever give her.

DECEMBER 30TH. Up and to the office, at noon home to dinner, and all the afternoon to my accounts, and there find myself, to my great joy, a great deal worth above £4,000, for which the Lord be praised! and is principally occasioned by my getting £500 of Cocke, for my profit in his bargains of prize goods, and from Mr. Gawden's making me a present of £500 more, when I paid him £8,000 for Tangier. So to my office to write letters, then to my accounts again, and so to bed, being in great ease of mind.

DECEMBER 31ST (Lord's Day). Thus ends this year, to my great joy, in this manner. I have raised my estate from £1,300 in this year to £4,400. I have got myself greater interest, I think, by my diligence, and my employments encreased by that of Treasurer for Tangier, and Surveyour of the Victualls. It is true we have gone through great melancholy because of the great plague. I have never lived so merry (besides that I never got so much) as I have done this plague time. My whole family hath been well all this while, and all my friends I know of, saving my aunt Bell, who is dead, and some children of my cozen Sarah's. Pray God continue the plague's decrease!

MARCH 31ST, 1666. All the morning at the office busy. At noon to dinner, and thence to the office and did my business there as soon as I could, and then home and to my accounts, where very late at them, but, Lord! what a deale of do I have to understand any part of them, and in short do what I could, I could not come to any understanding of them, but after I had thoroughly wearied myself, I was forced to go to bed and leave them much against my will and vowe too, but I hope God will forgive me, for I have sat up these four nights till past twelve at night to master them, but cannot. Thus ends this month, with my head and mind mighty full and disquiett because of my accounts, which I have let go too long, and confounded my publique with my private that I cannot come to any liquidating of them. However, I do see that I must be grown richer than I was by a good deale last month.

APRIL 3RD. After dinner I to my accounts hard all the afternoon till it was quite darke, and I thank God I do come to bring them very fairly to make me worth £5,000 stocke in the world, which is a great mercy to me.

AUGUST 1ST. Up betimes to the settling of my last month's accounts, and I bless God I find them very clear, and that I am worth £5,700, the most that ever my book did yet make out. So prepared to attend the Duke of Yorke as usual, but Sir W. Pen, just as I was going out, comes home from Sheernesse, and held me in discourse about publique business, till I come by coach too late to St. James's, and there find that everything stood still, and nothing done for want of me. Thence walked over the Parke with Sir W. Coventry. I left him going to Chappell, it being the common fast day. After dinner to Mrs. Martin's, and there find Mrs. Burroughs, and by and by comes a pretty widow, one Mrs. Eastwood, and one Mrs. Fenton, a maid; and here merry kissing and looking on their breasts, and all the innocent pleasure in the world. But, Lord! to see the dissembling of this widow, how upon the singing of a certain jigg by Doll, Mrs. Martin's sister, she seemed to be sick and fainted and God knows what, because the jigg which her husband (who died this last sickness) loved. But by and by I made her as merry as is possible.

OCTOBER 31ST. I have not been able to even my accounts since July last before; and I bless God that I do find that I am worth more than ever I yet was, which is £6,200, for which the Holy Name of God be praised!

DECEMBER 31ST. To dinner, and then to my accounts, wherein, at last, I find them clear and right, but to my great discontent do find that my gettings this year have been £573 less than my last: it being this year in all but £2,986. And then again, my spendings this year have exceeded my spendings the last by £644: my whole spendings last year being but £509; whereas this year, it appears, I have spent £1,154, which is a sum not fit to be said that ever I should spend in one year, before I am master of a better estate than I am. Yet, blessed be God! and I pray God make me thankful for it, I do find myself worth in money, all good, above £6,200. This, I trust in God, will make me thankfull for what I have, and careful to make up by care next year what by my negligence and prodigality I have lost and spent this year.

FEBRUARY 5TH, 1667. This morning, before I went to the office, there come to me Mr. Young and Whistler, flagg-makers, and with mighty earnestness did present me with, and press me to take a box, wherein I could not guess there was less than £100 in gold: but I do wholly refuse it, and did not at last take it. The truth is, not thinking them safe men to receive such a gratuity from, nor knowing any considerable courtesy that ever I did to them, but desirous to keep myself free from their reports, and to have it in my power to say I had refused their offer.

MAY 31ST. Late to supper, and with great quiet to bed; finding by the balance of my account that I am creditor £6,900, for which the Lord of Heaven be praised!

AUGUST 2ND. Away to the Office I went, where all the morning I was, only Mr. Gawden come to me, and he and I home to my chamber, and there reckoned, and there I received my profits for Tangier of him, and £250 on my victualling score. He is a most noble-minded man as ever I met with, and seems to own himself much obliged to me, which I will labour to make him; for he is a good man also: we talked on many good things relating to the King's service, and, in fine, I had much matter of joy by this morning's work, receiving above £400 of him on one account or other; and a promise that, though I lay down my victualling place, yet, as long as he continues victualler, I shall be the better by him.

## A SUNDAY IN THE COUNTRY

JULY 14TH, 1667 (Lord's Day). Up, and my wife, a little before four, and by and by Mrs. Turner come to us by agreement, and she and I stayed talking below while my wife dressed herself, which vexed me that she was so long about it, keeping us till past five o'clock before she was ready. She ready; and taking some bottles of wine and beer and cold fowle with us into the coach, we took coach and four horses, which I had provided last night, and so away. A very fine day, and so towards Epsum. The country very fine, only the way very dusty. We got to Epsum by eight o'clock, to the well; where much company, and there we 'light, and I drank the water: I did drink four pints. Here I met with divers of our town, among others with several of the tradesmen of our office, but did talk but little with them, it growing hot in the sun, and so we took coach again and to the towne, to the King's Head. Here we called for drink, and bespoke dinner; hear that my Lord Buckhurst and Nelly are lodged at the house. Poor girl! I pity her. W. Hewer rode with us, and I left him and the women, and myself walked to church, where few people, contrary to what I expected, and none I knew, but all the Houblons, brothers, and them after sermon

I did salute. They come last night to see their elder brother.
We parted to meet anon, and I to my women, and there to
dinner, a good dinner, and were merry, and Pendleton come
to us. After dinner, he gone, we all lay down (the day being
wonderful hot) to sleep, and each of us took a good nap, and
then rose. Took coach and to take the ayre, there being a fine
breeze. then I carried him to see my cozen Pepys's house, and
'light and walked round about it, and they like it, as indeed
it deserves, very well, and is a pretty place; and then I walked
them to the wood hard by, and there got them in the thickets
till they had lost themselves, and I could not find the way into
any of the walks in the wood, which indeed are very pleasant,
if I could have found them. At last got out of the wood again;
and I, by leaping down the little bank, coming out of the
wood, did sprain my right foot, which brought me great
present pain; but presently, with walking, it went away for the
present. And so the women and W. Hewer and I walked upon
the Downes, where a flock of sheep was; and the most pleasant
and innocent sight that ever I saw in my life. We find a
shepherd and his little boy reading, far from any houses or
sight of people, the Bible to him; so I made the boy read to
me, which he did, with the forced tone that children do
usually read, that was mighty pretty, and then I did give him
something, and went to the father and talked with him; and I
find he had been a servant in my cozen Pepys's house, and
told me what was become of their old servants. He did content himself mightily in my liking his boy's reading, and
did bless God for him the most like one of the old patriarchs
that ever I saw in my life, and it brought those thoughts of
the old age of the world in my mind for two or three days

after. We took notice of his woolen knit stockings of two colours mixed, and of his shoes shod with iron shoes, both at the toe and heels, and with great nails in the soles of his feet, which was mighty pretty: and, taking notice of them, "Why," says the poor man, "the downes, you see, are full of stones, and we are faine to shoe ourselves thus; and these," says he, "will make the stones fly till they sing before me." I did give the poor man something, for which he was mighty thankful, and I tried to cast stones with his horne crooke. He values his dog mightily, that would turn a sheep any way which he would have him when he goes to fold them: told me there was about eighteen scoare sheep in his flock, and that he hath four shillings a week the year round for keeping of them: so we posted thence with mighty pleasure in the discourse we had with this poor man, and Mrs. Turner, in the common fields here, did gather one of the prettiest nosegays that ever I saw in my life. So to our coach and through Mr. Minnes's wood, and looked upon Mr. Evelyn's house; and so over the common, and through Epsum towne to our inne, in the way stopping a poor woman with her milk-pail, and in one of my gilt tumblers did drink our bellyfulls of milk, better than any creame; and so to our inne and there had a dish of creame, but it was sour and so had no pleasure in it; and so paid our reckoning and took coach, it being about seven at night, and passed and saw the people walking with their wives and children to take the ayre; and we set out for home, the sun by and by going down, and we in the cool of the evening all the way with much pleasure home, talking and pleasing ourselves with the pleasure of this day's work. My foot begins more and more to pain me, which Mrs. Turner, by keeping her warm hand upon it, did much ease; but so that when we come home, which was just at eleven at night, I was not able to walk from the lane's end to my house without being helped, which did trouble me, and therefore to bed presently; but, thanks be to God, found that I had not been missed, nor any business happened in my absence. So to bed, and there had a cere-cloth laid to my foot and leg alone, but in great pain all night long.

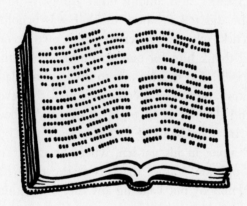

## PRAISE FOR PEPYS

OCTOBER 8TH, 1662. Up and by water to my Lord Sandwich's, and was with him a good while in his chamber, and among other things to my extraordinary joy, he did tell me how much I was beholding to the Duke of York, who did yesterday of his own accord tell him that he did thank him for one person brought into the Navy, naming myself, and much more to my commendation, which is the greatest comfort and encouragement that ever I had in my life, and do owe it all to Mr. Coventry's goodness.

APRIL 24TH, 1665. Walked an houre with my Lord Duke of Albemarle alone in his garden, where he expressed in great words his opinion of me; that I was the right hand of the Navy here, nobody but I taking any care of anything therein; so that he should not know what could be done without me. At which I was (from him) not a little proud. So by coach with my wife and Mercer to the Parke; but the King being there, and I now-a-days being doubtfull of being seen in any pleasure, did part from the tour, and away out of the Parke to Knightsbridge, and there eat and drank in the coach.

AUGUST 19TH. Our fleete is come home to our great grief with not above five weeks' dry, and six days' wet provisions:

however, must out again. Having read all this news, and received commands of the Duke with great content, he giving me the words which to my great joy he hath several times said to me that his greatest reliance is upon me. And my Lord Craven also did come out to talk with me, and told me that I am in mighty esteem with the Duke, for which I bless God.

JANUARY 28TH, 1666. And up again about six (Lord's Day), and so to my Lord Bruncker's with all my papers, and there took his coach with four horses and away toward Hampton Court. After dinner took coach and to Court, where we find the King, and Duke, and Lords, all in council. The Council being up, out comes the King, and I kissed his hand, and he grasped me very kindly by the hand. And the King come to me of himself, and told me, "Mr. Pepys," says he, "I do give you thanks for your good service all this year, and I assure you I am very sensible of it." And the Duke of Yorke did tell me with pleasure, that he had read over my discourse about pursers and would have it ordered in my way, and so fell from one discourse to another. I walked with them quite out of the Court into the fields.

FEBRUARY 14TH, 1667. At noon home to dinner, and after dinner by coach to my Lord Chancellor's, and there a meeting: the Duke of York, Duke of Albemarle, and several other Lords of the Commission of Tangier. And there I did present a state of my accounts, and managed them well; and my Lord Chancellor did say, though he was, in other things, in an ill humour, that no man in England was of more method, nor made himself better understood than myself.

APRIL 24TH. By coach to Sir John Duncomb's lodging in the Pell Mell, and there awhile sat and discoursed: and I find him that he is a very proper man for business, being very resolute and proud, and industrious. He told me what reformation they had made in the office of the Ordnance.

He says that he believes but four men (such as he could name) would do the business of both offices, his and ours, and if ever the war were to be again it should be so, he believes. He told me to my face that I was a very good clerk, and did understand the business and do it very well, and that he would never desire a better. He do believe that the Parliament, if ever they meet, will offer some alterations to the King, and will turn some of us out, and I protest I think he is in the right.

JUNE 27TH. Pierce tells me that all the town do cry out of our office for a pack of fools and knaves; but says that everybody speaks either well, or at least the best of me, which is my great comfort, and think I do deserve it, and shall shew I have; but yet do think, and he also, that the Parliament will send us all going; and I shall be well contented with it, God knows!

JULY 12TH. After dinner Sir Thomas Crew and I alone, and he tells me how I am mightily in esteem with the Parliament; there being harangues made in the House to the Speaker, of Mr. Pepys's readiness and civility to shew them every thing, which I am at this time very glad of.

DECEMBER 8TH (Lord's Day). I got my wife to read, and then come Captain Cocke to me; and there he tells me, to my great satisfaction, that Sir Robert Brookes did dine with him to-day; and that he told him, speaking of me, that he would make me the darling of the House of Commons, so much he is satisfied concerning me.

*The disastrous result of the Dutch War, and the bungling conduct of it, was a scandal through all England. There had been much rascally dishonesty among the public officers entrusted with the war's management, and Pepys had been chosen to render the accounting of the Navy Office to Parliament. The most clamorous complaint was that the seamen's wages were in arrears, and that some of them had been discharged with tickets, in lieu of money due them. For several nervous days Pepys prepared himself, and then the day came.*
—EDITOR.

MARCH 4TH, 1668. [Without] supper vexed and sickish to bed, and there slept about three hours, but then waked, and never in so much trouble in all my life of mind, thinking of the task I have upon me, and upon what dissatisfactory grounds, and what the issue of it may be to me.

MARCH 5TH. With these thoughts I lay troubling myself till six o'clock, restless, and at last getting my wife to talk to me to comfort me, which she at last did, and made me resolve to quit my hands of this Office, and endure the trouble of it no longer than till I can clear myself of it. So with great trouble, but yet with some ease, from this discourse with my wife, I up, and to my office, whither come my clerks, and so I did huddle, the best I could, some more notes for my discourse to-day, and by nine o'clock was ready, and did go down to the Old Swan, and there by boat, with T. H. and W. H. with me, to Westminster, were I found myself come time enough, and my brethren all ready. But I full of thoughts and trouble touching the issue of this day; and, to comfort myself did go to the Dog and drink half-a-pint of mulled sack, and in the Hall did drink

a dram of brandy at Mrs. Hewlett's; and with the warmth of
this did find myself in better order as to courage, truly. So we
all up to the lobby; and between eleven and twelve o'clock,
were called in, with the mace before us, into the House, where
a mighty full House; and we stood at the bar, namely,
Brouncker, Sir J. Minnes, Sir T. Harvey and myself, W. Pen
being in the House, as a member. I perceive the whole House
was full, and full of expectation of our defense, what it would
be, and with great prejudice. After the Speaker had told us
the dissatisfaction of the House, and read the Report of the
Committee, I began our defense most acceptably and smoothly,
and continued at it without any hesitation or losse, but with
full scope, and all my reason free about me as if it had been at
my own table, from that time till past three in the afternoon,
and so ended, without any interruption from the Speaker; but
we withdrew. And there all my Fellow-Officers, and all the
world that was within hearing, did congratulate me, and cry
up my speech as the best thing they ever heard; and my
Fellow-Officers overjoyed in it; we were called in again by and
by to answer only one question, touching our paying tickets to
ticket-mongers; and so out; and we were in hopes to have had
a vote this day in our favour, and so the generality of the
House was; but my speech, being so long, many had gone out
to dinner and come in again half-drunk; and then there are
two or three that are professed enemies to us and every body
else; among others Sir T. Littleton and a few others; I say,
these did rise up and speak against the coming to a vote now,
the House not being full; so that they put it off to to-morrow
come se'nnight. However, it is plain we have got great
ground; and every body says I have got the most honour that

any could have had opportunity of getting; and so with our hearts mightily overjoyed at this success, we all to dinner to Lord Brouncker's—that is to say, myself, T. Harvey, and W. Pen, and there dined.

MARCH 6TH. Up betimes, and with Sir D. Gawden to Sir W. Coventry's Chamber, where the first word he said to me was, "Good-morrow, Mr. Pepys, that must be Speaker of the Parliament-house:" and did protest I had got honour for ever in Parliament. He said that his brother, that sat by him, admires me; and another gentleman said that I could not get less than £1,000 a-year if I would put on a gown and plead at the Chancery-bar; but, what pleases me most, he tells me that the Sollicitor-Generall did protest that he thought I spoke the best of any man in England. After several talks with him alone, touching his own businesses, he carried me to White Hall, and there parted; and I to the Duke of York's lodgings, and find him going to the Park, it being a very fine morning, and I after him; and, as soon as he saw me, he told me, with great satisfaction, that I had converted a great many yesterday, and did, with great praise of me, go on with the discourse with me. And, by and by, overtaking the King, the King and Duke of York come to me both; and he said, "Mr. Pepys, I am very glad of your success yesterday;" and fell to talk of my well-speaking; and many of the Lords there. My Lord Barkeley did cry me up for what they had heard of it; and others, Parliament-men there, about the King, did say that they never heard such a speech in their lives delivered in that manner. Progers, of the Bedchamber, swore to me afterwards before Brouncker, in the afternoon, that he did tell the King that he thought I might teach the Sollicitor-Generall. Every body that saw me almost come to me, as Joseph Williamson and others, with such eulogys as cannot be expressed. From thence I went to Westminster Hall, where I met Mr. G. Montagu, who come to me and kissed me, and told me that he had often heretofore kissed my hands, but now he would kiss my lips: protesting that I was another Cicero, and said, all the world said the same of me. Mr. Ashburnham, and every creature I met there of the Parliament, or that knew anything of the Parliament's actings, did salute me with this honour:— Mr. Godolphin;—Mr. Sands, who swore he would go twenty mile, at any time, to hear the like again, and that he never saw so many sit four hours together to hear any man in his life, as there did to hear me; Mr. Chichly,—Sir John Duncomb,—and every body do say that the kingdom will ring of my abilities, and that I have done myself right for my whole life: and so Captain Cocke, and others of my friends, say that no man had ever such an opportunity of making his abilities known; and, that I may cite all at once, Mr. Lieutenant of the Tower did tell me that Mr. Vaughan did protest to him, and that, in his hearing it, said so to the Duke of Albemarle, and afterwards to W. Coventry, that he had sat twenty-six years in Parliament and never heard such a speech there before: for which the Lord God make me thankful! and that I may make use of it not to pride and vain-glory, but that, now I have this esteem, I may do nothing that may lessen it! I spent the morning thus walking in the Hall, being complimented by everybody with admiration.

MARCH 30TH, 1669. Up, and to Sir W. Coventry, to see and discourse with him; and he tells me that he hath lately been with my Lord Keeper, and had much discourse about the

Navy; and particularly he tells me that he finds they are divided touching me and my Lord Brouncker; some are for removing, and some for keeping us. He told my Lord Keeper that it would cost the King £10,000 before he hath made another as fit to serve him in the Navy as I am; which, though I believe it is true, yet I am much pleased to have that character given me by W. Coventry, whatever be the success of it. But I perceive they do think that I know too much, and shall impose upon whomever shall come next, and therefore must be removed. This news do a little trouble me, but yet, when I consider it, it is but what I ought not to be much troubled for, considering my incapacity, in regard to my eyes. After some talk of the business of the navy more with him, I away and to the Office, where all the morning; and Sir W. Pen, the first time that he hath been here since his being sick, which, I think, is two or three months; and I think will be the last, which I am glad of, I am sure; for he is a very villain.

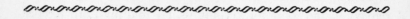

# ARITHMETIC IN THE SEVENTEENTH CENTURY *

JULY 4TH, 1662. Up by five o'clock, and after my journall put in order, to my office about my business, which I am resolved to follow, for every day I see what ground I get by it. By and by comes Mr. Cooper, mate of the Royall Charles, of whom I intend to learn mathematiques, and do begin with him to-day, he being a very able man, and no great matter, I suppose, will content him. After an hour's being with him at arithmetique (my first attempt being to learn the multiplication-table); then we parted till to-morrow. And so to my business at my office again till noon.

JULY 9TH. Up by four o'clock, and at my multiplicacion-table hard, which is all the trouble I meet withal in my arithmetique. So made me ready and to the office. Then to my business till night, then Mr. Cooper and I to our business, and then come Mr. Mills, the minister, to see me, which he hath but rarely done to me, though every day almost to others of us; but he is a cunning fellow, and knows where the good victuals is, and the good drink, at Sir W. Batten's. However, I used him civilly, though I love him as I do the rest of his coat. So to supper and to bed.

* See and compare with *A Glimpse at Higher Education,* noting the dates.

JULY 11TH. Up by four o'clock and hard at my multiplicacion-table, which I am now almost master of.

JULY 12TH. Up by five o'clock, and put things in my house in order to be laid up. So to my office, where till noon we sat, and then I to dinner and to the office all afternoon with much business. At night with Cooper at arithmetique, and then came Mr. Creed about my Lord's accounts to even them, and he gone I to supper and to bed.

JULY 14TH. Up by four o'clock and to my arithmetique, and so to my office till 8, then to Thames Street along with old Mr. Green, among the tarr-men, and did instruct myself in the nature and prices of tarr, but could not get Stockholm for the use of the office under £10 15s.

OCTOBER 21ST, 1663. This evening after I came home I begun to enter my wife in arithmetique, in order to her studying of the globes, and she takes it very well, and, I hope, with great pleasure, I shall bring her to understand many fine things.

SEPTEMBER 29TH, 1664. Coming home to-night, I did go to examine my wife's house accounts, and finding things that seemed somewhat doubtful, I was angry though she did make it pretty plain, but confessed that when she do misse a sum, she do add something to other things to make it, and, upon my being very angry she do protest she will here lay up something for herself to buy a necklace with, which madded me and do still trouble me, for I fear she will forget by degrees the way of living cheap and under sense of want.

## INCIDENTS OF MATCHMAKING

JUNE 23RD, 1665. My Lord did begin to tell me how much he was concerned to dispose of his children, and would have my advice and help; and propounded to match my Lady Jemimah to Sir G. Carteret's eldest son, which I approved of, and did undertake the speaking with him about it as from myself, which my Lord liked. So parted.

JUNE 24TH. Up, and at Dr. Clerke's at Westminster by 7 of the clock, and there I broke my errand about a match between Sir G. Carteret's eldest son and my Lord Sandwich's eldest daughter; and he did undertake to find out Sir George this morning, and put the business in execution. [*Later in the day Pepys learns that Dr. Clerke has seen Sir George.*—EDITOR.] Thence I to Sir G. Carteret at his chamber, and in the best manner I could, and most obligingly, moved the business: he received it with great respect and content, and thanks to me, and promised that he would do what he could possibly for his son, to render him fit for my Lord's daughter, and shewed great kindness to me, and sense of my kindness to him herein. Sir William Pen told me this day that Mr. Coventry is to be sworn a Privy Counsellor, at which my soul is glad. So home.

JUNE 25TH (Lord's Day). Through bridge to White Hall,

where, after I had again visited Sir G. Carteret, and received his (and now his Lady's) full content in my proposal, I went to my Lord Sandwich, and having told him how Sir G. Carteret received it, he did direct me to return to Sir G. Carteret, and give him thanks for his kind reception of this offer, and that he would the next day be willing to enter discourse with him about the business. Which message I did presently do, and so left the business with great joy to both sides. My Lord, I perceive, intends to give £5,000 with her, and expects about £800 per *annum* joynture. So by water home and to supper and bed, being weary with long walking at Court, but had a Psalm or two with my boy and Mercer before bed.

JUNE 28TH. This morning I met with Sir G. Carteret, who tells me how all things proceed between my Lord Sandwich and himself to full content, and both sides depend upon having the match finished presently, and professed great kindnesse to me, and said that now we were something akin. I am mightily, both with respect to myself and much more of my Lord's family, glad of this alliance. My Lord Sandwich is gone towards the sea to-day, it being a sudden resolution.

JULY 5TH. To White Hall to Sir G. Carteret, who is come this day from Chatham, and mighty glad he is to see me, and begun to talk of our great business of the match, which goes on as fast as possible, but for convenience we took water and over to his coach to Lambeth, by which we went to Deptford, all the way talking, first, how matters are quite concluded with all possible content between my Lord and him and signed and sealed, so that my Lady Sandwich is to come thither to-morrow or next day, and the young lady is sent for, and all likely to be ended between them in a very little while, with mighty joy on both sides, and the King, Duke, Lord Chancellor, and all mightily pleased. Being come to Deptford, I by water to Woolwich, where I found my wife come, and her two mayds, and very prettily accommodated they will be; and I left them going to supper, grieved in my heart to part with my wife, being worse by much without her. Late home and to bed, very lonely.

JULY 9TH (Lord's Day). We are received with most extraordinary kindnesse by my Lady Carteret and her children, and dined most nobly. Sir G. Carteret went to Court this morning. After dinner I took occasion to have much discourse with Mr. Ph. Carteret, and find him a very modest man; and I think verily of mighty good nature, and pretty understanding. He did give me a good account of the fight with the Dutch. My Lady Sandwich dined in her chamber. About three o'clock I, leaving my wife there, took boat and home, and there shifted myself into my black silke suit, and having promised Harman yesterday, I to his house, which I find very mean.

JULY 14TH. In the evening, I by water to Sir G. Carteret's, and there find my Lady Sandwich and her buying things for my Lady Jem.'s wedding; and my Lady Jem. is beyond expectation come to Dagenhams, where Mr. Carteret is to go to visit her to-morrow; and my proposal of waiting on him, he being to go alone to all persons strangers to him, was well accepted, and so I go with him. But, Lord! to see how kind my Lady Carteret is to her! Sends her most rich jewells, and provides bedding and things of all sorts most richly for her, which makes my Lady and me out of our wits almost to see the kindnesse she treats us all with, as if they would buy the young lady. Thence away home and, foreseeing my being abroad two days, did sit up late making of letters ready against to-morrow, and other things, and so to bed, to be up betimes by the helpe of a larum watch, which by chance I borrowed of my watchmaker to-day, while my owne is mending.

JULY 15TH. By boat to Redriffe, and thence walked, and after dinner at Sir G. Carteret's, where they stayed till almost three o'clock for me, and anon took boat, Mr. Carteret and I, and so toward Dagenhams. But, Lord! what silly discourse we had by the way as to love-matters, he being the most awkerd man I ever met with in my life as to that business. Thither we come, by that time it begun to be dark, and were kindly received by Lady Wright and my Lord Crew. And to discourse they went, my Lord discoursing with him, asking of him questions of travell, which he answered well enough in a few words; but nothing to the lady from him at all. To supper, and after supper to talk again, he yet taking no notice of the lady. My Lord would have had me have consented to leaving the young people together to-night, to begin their amours, his staying being but to be little. But I advised against it, lest the lady might be too surprised. So they led him up to his chamber, where I staid a little, to know how he liked the lady, which he told me he did mightily; but, Lord! in the dullest insipid manner that ever lover did. So I bid him good-night, and after prayers, my Lord, and Lady Wright, and I, to consult what to do; and it was agreed at last to have them go to church together, as the family used to do.

JULY 16TH (Lord's Day). I up, having lain with Mr. Moore in the chaplin's chamber. And having trimmed myself, down to Mr. Carteret; and he being ready we down and walked in the gallery an hour or two, it being a most noble and pretty house that ever, for the bigness, I saw. Here I taught him what to do: to take the lady always by the hand to lead her, and telling him that I would find opportunity to leave them two together, he should make these and these compliments, and also take a time to do the like to Lord Crew and Lady Wright. After I had instructed him, which he thanked me for, owning that he needed my teaching him, my Lord Crew come down and family, the young lady among the rest; and so by coaches to church four miles off; where a pretty good sermon, and a declaration of penitence of a man that had undergone the Churche's censure for his wicked life. Thence back again by coach, Mr. Carteret having not had the confidence to take his lady once by the hand, coming or going, which I told him of when we come home, and he will hereafter do it. So to dinner. My Lord excellent discourse. Then to walk in the gallery, and to sit down. By and by my Lady Wright and I go out (and then my Lord Crew, he not by design), and lastly my Lady Crew come out, and left the young people together. And a little pretty daughter of my Lady Wright's most innocently come out afterward, and shut the door to, as if she had done it, poor child, by inspiration; which made us without, have good sport to laugh at. They together an hour, and by and by church-time, whither he led her into the coach and into the church, and so at church all the afternoon, several handsome ladies at church. But it was most extraordinary hot that ever I knew it. So home again and to walk in the gardens, where we left the young couple a second time; and my Lady Wright and I to walk together, who to my trouble tells me that my Lady Jem. must have something done to her body by Scott before she can be married, and therefore care must be had to

send him, also that some more new clothes must of necessity
be made her, which and other things I took care of. Anon to
supper, and excellent discourse and dispute between my Lord
Crew and the chaplin, who is a good scholler, but a noncon-
formist. After Mr. Carteret was carried to his chamber, we to
prayers again and then to bed.

July 17th. Up all of us, and to billiards; my Lady Wright,
Mr. Carteret, myself, and every body. By and by the young
couple left together. Anon to dinner; and after dinner Mr.
Carteret took my advice about giving to the servants, and I
led him to give £10 among them, which he did, by leaving it
to the chief man-servant, Mr. Medows, to do for him. Before
we went, I took my Lady Jem. apart, and would know how
she liked this gentleman, and whether she was under any difficulty concerning him. She blushed, and hid her face awhile;
but at last I forced her to tell me. She answered that she
could readily obey what her father and mother had done;
which was all she could say, or I expect. So anon I took leave,
and for London. In our way Mr. Carteret did give me mighty
thanks for my care and pains for him, and is mightily pleased,
though the truth is, my Lady Jem. hath carried herself with
mighty discretion and gravity, not being forward at all in any
degree.

July 28th. Up betimes, and down to Deptford, where, after
a little discourse with Sir G. Carteret, set out with my Lady
all alone with her with six horses to Dagenhams; going by
water to the Ferry. And a pleasant going, and good discourse;
and when there, very merry, and the young people now well
acquainted. But, Lord! to see in what fear all the people here
do live would make one mad, they are afeard of us that come

to them, insomuch that I am troubled at it, and wish myself away. [*An epidemic of the plague was raging in London at the time, and thence Pepys had come.*—Editor.] But some cause they have; for the chaplin, with whom but a week or two ago we were here mighty highly disputing, is since fallen into a fever and dead, being gone hence to a friend's a good way off. A sober and healthful man. These considerations make us all hasten the marriage, and resolve it upon Monday next, which is three days before we intended it. Mighty merry all of us, and in the evening with full content took coach again and home by daylight with great pleasure, and thence I down to Woolwich, where find my wife well, and after drinking and talking a little we to bed.

July 31st. Up, and very betimes by six o'clock at Deptford, and there find Sir G. Carteret, and my Lady ready to go: I being in my new coloured silk suit, and coat trimmed with gold buttons and gold broad lace round my hands, very rich and fine. By water to the Ferry, where, when we come, no coach there; and tide of ebb so far spent as the horse-boat could not get off on the other side the river to bring away the coach. So we were fain to stay there in the unlucky Isle of Doggs, in a chill place, the morning cool, and wind fresh, above two if not three hours to our great discontent. Yet being upon a pleasant errand, and seeing that it could not be helped, we did bear it very patiently; and Sir G. Carteret, the most passionate man in the world, did bear with it, and very pleasant all the while. Anon the coach comes. We, fearing the canonicall hour would be past before we got thither, did with a great deal of unwillingness send away the license and wedding ring. So that when we come, though we drove hard with six horses,

yet we found them gone from home; and going towards the church, met them coming from church, which troubled us. But, however, that trouble was soon over; hearing it was well done. The young lady mighty sad, which troubled me; but yet I think it was only her gravity in a little greater degree than usual. All saluted her, but I did not till my Lady Sandwich did ask me whether I had saluted her or no. So to dinner, and very merry we were; but yet in such a sober way as never almost any wedding was in so great families: but it was much better. At night to supper, and so to talk; and which, me-thought, was the most extraordinary thing, all of us to prayers as usual, and the young bride and bridegroom too: and so after prayers, soberly to bed; only I got into the bridegroom's chamber while he undressed himself, and there was very merry, till he was called to the bride's chamber, and into bed they went. I kissed the bride in bed, and so the curtaines drawn with the greatest gravity that could be, and so good night. But the modesty and gravity of this business was so decent, that it was to me indeed ten times more delightfull than if it had been twenty times more merry and joviall. Thus I ended this month with the greatest joy that ever I did any in my life, because I have spent the greatest part of it with abundance of joy, and honour, and pleasant journeys, and brave entertainments, and without cost of money; and at last live to see the business ended with great content on all sides.

AUGUST 1ST. Slept and lay long; then up and my Lord and Sir G. Carteret being gone abroad, I first to see the bridegroom and bride, and found them both up, and he gone to dress himself. Both red in the face, and well enough pleased this morning with their night's lodging. I left them, and home to the office, where I find all well.

*Elapsed time, forty days. Mr. Pepys handled this very expeditiously. Something more than two years later, he had a more troublesome affair on his hands.*—EDITOR.

OCTOBER 10TH, 1667. Rose, and up to walk up and down the garden with my father, to talk of all our concernments: about a husband for my sister, whereof there is at present no appearance; but we must endeavour to find her one now, for she grows old and ugly.*

NOVEMBER 19TH. This night I wrote to my father, in answer to a new match which is proposed (the executor of Ensum, my sister's former servant) for my sister, that I will continue my mind of giving her £500, if he likes of the match.

DECEMBER 21ST. I to the office, where busy till late at night, and then home to sit with my wife, who is a little better, and her cheek asswaged. I read to her out of "The History of Algiers," which is mighty pretty reading, and did discourse alone about my sister Pall's match, which is now on foot with one Jackson, another nephew of Mr. Phillips's, to whom he hath left his estate.

JANUARY 10TH, 1668. This day I received a letter from my father, and another from my cozen Roger Pepys, who have had a view of Jackson's evidences of his estate, and do advise me to accept of the match for my sister, and to finish it as soon as I can; and he do it so as, I confess, I am contented to have it done, and so give her her portion; and so I shall be eased of one care how to provide for her.

* Paulina Pepys was born in 1640.

FEBRUARY 7TH. I away first to Westminster Hall, and there met my cozen, Roger Pepys, by his desire, and here he tells me that Mr. Jackson, my sister's servant, is come to town, in order to the making her a settlement. The young man is gone out of the Hall, so I could not now see him, but here I walked a good while with my cozen. Thence to the Commissioners of Accounts, and there presented my books, and was made to sit down, and used with much respect, otherwise than the other day. Thence I about two o'clock, to Westminster Hall, by appointment, and there met my cozen Roger again, and Mr. Jackson, who is a plain young man, handsome enough for Pall, one of no education nor discourse, but of few words, and one altogether that, I think, will please me well enough. My cozen had got me to give the odd sixth £100 presently, which I intended to keep to the birth of the first child; and let it go—I shall be eased of the care, and so, after little talk, we parted, resolving to dine together at my house to-morrow. So there parted, my mind pretty well satisfied with this plain fellow for my sister, though I shall, I see, have no content in him, as if he had been a man of reading and parts.

FEBRUARY 10TH. I to Westminster Hall, and there met Roger Pepys, and with him to his chamber, and there read over and agreed upon the Deed of Settlement to our minds: my sister to have £600 presently, and she to be joyntured in £60 per annum; wherein I am very well satisfied.

MARCH 2ND. This day I have the news that my sister was married on Thursday last to Mr. Jackson; so that work is, I hope, well over.

MAY 24TH. I up, at between two and three in the morning, and, calling up my boy, and father's boy, we set out by three o'clock, it being high day; and so through the waters with very good success, though very deep almost all the way, and got to Brampton. Here I saw my brothers and sister Jackson, she growing fat, and, since being married, I think looks comelier than before: but a mighty pert woman she is, and I think proud, he keeping her mighty handsome, and they say mighty fond, and are going shortly to live at Ellington of themselves, and will keep malting, and grazing of cattle.

MAY 12TH, 1669. My brother John come to town from Ellington, where, among other things, he tells me the first news that my [sister Jackson] is with child, and far gone, which I know not whether it did more trouble or please me, having no great care for my friends to have children, though I love other people's. So, glad to see him, we to supper, and so to bed.

## THE PLAGUE

OCTOBER 19TH, 1663. Sir W. Batten and I took coach, and to the Coffee-house in Cornhill; where much talk about the Turk's proceedings, and that the plague is got to Amsterdam; and it is also carried to Hambrough. The Duke says the King purposes to forbid any of their ships coming into the river.

NOVEMBER 26TH. The plague, it seems, grows more and more at Amsterdam; and we are going upon making of all ships coming from thence and Hambrough, or any other infected places, to perform their Quarantine.

*With such mention, the theme of the plague recurs at intervals in the diary for something less than two years. Then Pepys and his family find it in their own community.*—EDITOR.

APRIL 30TH, 1665. Great fears of the sicknesse here in the City, it being said that two or three houses are already shut up. God preserve us all!

JUNE 7TH. This day, much against my will, I did in Drury Lane see two or three houses marked with a red cross upon the doors, and "Lord have mercy upon us" writ there; which was a sad sight to me, being the first of the kind that, to my remembrance, I ever saw. It put me into an ill conception of myself and my smell, so that I was forced to buy some roll-tobacco to smell and to chaw.

JUNE 20TH. This day I informed myself that there died four or five at Westminster of the plague in one alley in several houses upon Sunday last, Bell Alley, over against the palace gate; yet people do think that the number will be fewer in the towne than it was last week.

JUNE 21ST. So homeward and to the Cross Keys at Cripplegate, where I find all the towne almost going out of the towne, the coaches and waggons being all full of people going into the country. Here I had some of the company of the tapster's wife a while, and so home to my office, and then home to supper and to bed.

JULY 30TH (Lord's Day). It was a sad noise to hear our bell to toll and ring so often to-day, either for deaths or burials; I think five or six times.

AUGUST 31ST. Up; and, after putting several things in order to my removal, to Woolwich; the plague having a great encrease this week, beyond all expectation of almost 2,000, making the generall Bill 7,000, odd 100; and the plague above 6,000. Thus this month ends with great sadness upon the publick, through the greatness of the plague every where throughout the kingdom, almost. In the City died this week 7,496, and of them 6,102 of the plague. But it is feared that the true number of the dead this week is near 10,000; partly from the poor that cannot be taken notice of through the greatness of the number, and partly from the Quakers and others that will not have any bell ring for them. Our fleete gone out to find the Dutch; all our fear is that the Dutch should be got in before them, which would be a very great sorrow to the publick, and to me particularly for my Lord Sandwich's sake. A great deal of money being spent, and the kingdom not in a condition to spare, nor a parliament without much difficulty to meet to give more. As to myself I am very well, only in fear of the plague, and as much of an ague by being forced to go early and late to Woolwich, and my family to lie there continually.

SEPTEMBER 19TH. What a sad time it is to see no boats upon the River; and grass grows all up and down White Hall court, and nobody but poor wretches in the streets!

OCTOBER 5TH. The Bill, blessed be God! is less this week by 740 of what it was the last week. Being come to my lodging I got something to eat, having eat little all the day, and so to bed, having this night renewed my promises of observing my vowes as I used to do; for I find, that since I left them off, my mind is run a-wool-gathering and my business neglected.

OCTOBER 16TH. Lord! How empty the streets are and melancholy, so many poor sick people in the streets full of sores; and so many sad stories overheard as I walk, every body talking of this dead, and that man sick, and so many in this place, and so many in that. And they tell me that, in Westminster, there is never a physician and but one apothecary left, all being dead; but that there are great hopes of a great decrease this week: God send it!

NOVEMBER 30TH. Great joy we have this week in the weekly Bill, it being come to 544 in all, and but 333 of the plague; so that we are encouraged to get to London as soon as we can. And my father writes as great news of joy to them, that he saw Yorke's waggon go again this week to London, and was full of passengers.

JANUARY 5TH, 1666. I with my Lord Bruncker and Mrs. Williams by coach with four horses to London, to my Lord's house in Covent-Guarden. But, Lord! what staring to see a nobleman's coach come to town. And porters every where bow to us; and such begging of beggars! And a delightfull thing it is to see the towne full of people again as it now is; and shops begin to open, though in many places seven or eight together, and more, all shut; but yet the towne is full, compared with what it used to be. I mean the City end; for Covent-Guarden and Westminster are yet very empty of people, no Court nor gentry being there. I met Mr. Povy newly come to town, and he and I to Sir George Smith's and there dined nobly. We had no time to talk of particulars, and I away to Cornhill to expect my Lord Bruncker's coming back again, and I staid at my stationer's house, and by and by comes my Lord, and did take me up and so to Greenwich, and after sitting with them a while at their house, home, thinking to get Mrs. Knipp, but could not, she being busy with company, but sent me a pleasant letter, writing herself "Barbary Allen." So home and to my papers for lacke of company, but by and by comes little Mrs. Tooker and sat and supped with me, and I kept her very late talking and making her comb my head.

⤜⤚⤜⤚⤜⤚⤜⤚⤜⤚⤜⤚⤜⤚⤜⤚⤜⤚⤜⤚⤜⤚⤜⤚⤜⤚⤜⤚

## A DREAM TAKES FORM

MARCH 2ND, 1662 (Lord's Day). With my mind much eased talking long in bed with my wife about our frugall life for the time to come, proposing to her what I could and would do if I were worth £2,000, that is, be a knight, and keep my coach, which pleased her.

*Rising fortune and "frugall" living made Pepys worth more than £6,900 before we find another remark on the subject.* —EDITOR.

JUNE 1ST. Up; and there comes to me Mr. Commander, whom I employ about hiring of some ground behind the office, for the building of me a stable and coach-house: for I do find it necessary for me, both in respect to honour and the profit of it also, my expense in hackney-coaches being now so great, to keep a coach, and therefore will do it.

JULY 14TH (Lord's Day). Saw the people walking with their wives and children to take the ayre, and we set out for home, the sun by and by going down, and we in the cool of the evening all the way with much pleasure home, talking and pleasing ourselves with the pleasure of this day's work,

Mrs. Turner mightily pleased with my resolution, which, I tell her, is never to keep a country-house, but to keep a coach, and with my wife on the Saturday to go sometimes for a day to this place, and then quit to another place; and there is more variety and as little charge, and no trouble, as there is in a country-house. Anon it grew dark, and as it grew dark we had the pleasure to see several glow-wormes, which was mighty pretty. We come home just at eleven at night.

AUGUST 24TH. After dinner we to a play, and there saw "The Cardinall" at the King's house. So with my wife to Mile End, and there drank of Bide's ale, and so home. Most of our discourse is about our keeping a coach the next year, which pleases my wife mightily; and if I continue as able as now it will save us money.

MARCH 1ST, 1668 (Lord's Day). Home, and there my mind being a little lightened by my morning's work in the arguments I have now laid together in better method for our defence to the Parliament, I to talk with my wife; and in lieu of a coach this year I have got my wife to be contented with her closet being made up this summer, and going into the country this summer for a month or two, to my father's, and there Mercer and Deb. and Jane shall go with her.

OCTOBER 20TH. This day a new girl come to us in the room of Nell, who is lately, about four days since, gone away, being growing lazy and proud. This girl to stay only until we have a boy, which I intend to keep when we have a coach, which I am now about. At this time my wife and I mighty busy laying out money in dressing up our best chamber, and thinking of a coach and coachman and horses, &c.; and the more because of Creed's being now married to Mrs. Pickering; a thing I could never have expected, but done about seven or ten days since. At noon home to dinner, and my wife and Harman and girl abroad to buy things, and I walked out to several places to pay debts, and among other things to look out for a coach, and saw many; and did light on one for which I bid £50, which do please me mightily, and I believe I shall have it. So to my tailor's.

OCTOBER 21ST. To the New Exchange and there staid for my wife, and she come, we to Cow Lane, and there I shewed her the coach which I pitch on, and she is out of herself for joy almost. But the man not within, so did nothing more towards an agreement.

OCTOBER 24TH. This morning comes to me the coachmaker, and agreed with me for £53, and stand to the courtesy of what more I should give him upon the finishing of the coach: he is likely also to fit me with a coachman. There comes also to me Mr. Shotgrave, to show me his method of making the Tubes for the eyes.

NOVEMBER 5TH. With Mr. Povy spent all the afternoon going up and down among the coachmakers in Cow Lane, and did see several, and at last did pitch upon a little chariott, whose body was framed, but not covered, at the widow's, that made Mr. Lowther's fine coach; and we are mightily pleased with it, it being light, and will be very genteel and sober: to be covered with leather, and yet will hold four. Much satisfied with this.

NOVEMBER 23RD. I took up my wife and boy to Unthank's and from there to Hercules Pillars and there dined, and so to see our coach, and so to the looking-glass man's by the

New Exchange, and so to buy a picture for our blue chamber chimney, and so home.

NOVEMBER 28TH. Up, and all the morning at the Office, where, while I was sitting, one comes and tells me that my coach is come. So I was forced to go out and to Sir Richard Ford's, where I spoke to him, and he is very willing to have it brought in, and stand there; and so I ordered it, to my great content, it being mighty pretty, only the horses do not please me, and therefore resolve to have better.

NOVEMBER 29TH. This morning my coachman's clothes come home, and I like the livery mightily. I told [Sir W. Warren] it was now manifestly for my profit to keep a coach, and that, after employments like mine for eight years it were hard if I could not be justly thought to be able to do that.

DECEMBER 3RD. To the Duke of York's playhouse. We sat under the boxes, and saw the fine ladies, among others, my Lady Kerneguy, who is most devilishly painted. And so home, it being mighty pleasure to go alone with my poor wife, in a coach of our own, to a play, and makes us appear mighty great, I think, in the world; at least, greater than ever I could, or my friends for me, have once expected; or, I think, than ever any of my family ever yet lived, in my memory, but my cozen Pepys in Salisbury Court. So to the office, and thence home to supper and to bed.

APRIL 11TH, 1669. I took my wife to St. James's, and there carried her to the Queen's Chapel, the first time I ever did it. Thence to the Park, my wife and I; and here Sir W. Coventry did first see me and my wife in a coach of our own; and so did also the Duke of York, who did eye my wife mightily. But I begin to doubt that my being so much seen in my own coach at this time, may be observed to my prejudice; but I must venture it now. So home to supper and to bed.

MAY 1ST. My wife extraordinary fine, and mighty earnest to go, though the day was very lowering. And so anon we went alone through the town with our new liveries of serge, and the horses' manes and tails tied with red ribbons, and the standards there gilt with varnish, and all clean, and green reines, that people did mightily look upon us; and, the truth is, I did not see any coach more pretty, though more gay, than ours, all the day. The Park full of coaches, but dusty and windy and cold, and now and then a little dribbling rain; and what made it worst, there were so many hackney-coaches as spoiled the sight of the gentlemen's, and so we had little pleasure.

## SCIENCE AND INVENTION

OCTOBER 11th, 1660. Mr. Creed and I to dinner, and from thence to walk in St. James's Park, where we observed the several engines at work to draw up water, with which sight I was very much pleased. Above the rest, I liked best that which Mr. Greatorex brought, which is one round thing going within all with a pair of stairs round; round which being laid at an angle of 45°, do carry up the water with a great deal of ease. Here, in the Park, we met with Mr. Salisbury, who took Mr. Creed and me to the Cockpitt to see "The Moore of Venice," which was well done.

JUNE 9th, 1663. Up and after ordering some things towards my wife's going into the country, to the office, where I spent the morning upon my measuring rules very pleasantly till noon, and then comes Creed and he and I talked about mathematiques, and he tells me of a way found out by Mr. Jonas Moore which he calls duodecimal arithmetique, which is properly applied to measuring, where all is ordered by inches, which are 12 in a foot, which I have a mind to learn. So he with me home to dinner.

JULY 31ST. Before I went to the office I went to the Coffee House, where Sir J. Cutler and Mr. Grant were, and there Mr. Grant showed me letters of Sir William Petty's, wherein he says that his vessel which he hath built upon two keeles (a modell whereof, built for the King, he showed me) hath this month won a wager of £50 in sailing between Dublin and Holyhead with the pacquett-boat, the best ship or vessel the King hath there; and he offers to lay with any vessel in the world. It is about thirty ton in burden, and carries thirty men, with good accommodation (as much more as any ship of her burden), and so any vessel of this figure shall carry more men, with better accommodation by half, than shall any other ship. This carries also ten guns, of about five tons weight. Strange things are told of this vessel, and he concludes his letter with this position, "I can only affirm that the perfection of sayling lies in my principle, finde it out who can."

AUGUST 7TH. Up and to my office a little, and then to Brown's for my measuring rule, which is made, and is certainly the best and the most commodious for carrying in one's pocket, and most useful that ever was made, and myself have the honour of being as it were the inventor of this form of it. So home, and my brother John and I up and I to my musique, and then to discourse with him, and I find him not so thorough a philosopher, at least in Aristotle, as I took him for, he not being able to tell me the definition of final nor which of the 4 Qualitys belonging to each of the 4 Elements. So to bed.

AUGUST 8TH. Asking many things in physiques of my brother John, to which he gives me so bad or no answer at all, as in the regions of the ayre he told me that he knew of no such thing, for he never read Aristotle's philosophy and Des Cartes ownes no such thing, which vexed me to hear him say. But I shall call him to task, and see what it is that he has studied since his going to the University.

SEPTEMBER 8TH. Abroad, and among other places to Moxon's and there bought a payre of globes cost me £3 10s., with which I am well pleased, I buying them principally for my wife, who has a mind to understand them, and I shall take pleasure to teach her. But here I saw his great window in his dining room, where there is the two Terrestrial Hemispheres, so painted as I never saw in my life, and nobly done and to good purpose, done by his own hand.

FEBRUARY 1ST, 1664. To White Hall; where, in the Duke's chamber, the King came and stayed an hour or two laughing at Sir W. Petty, who was there about his boat; and at Gresham College in general; at which poor Petty was, I perceive, at some loss; but did argue discreetly, and bear the unreasonable follies of the King's objections and other bystanders with great discretion; and offered to take oddes against the King's best boates; but the King would not lay, but cried him down with words only. Gresham College he mightily laughed at, for spending time only in weighing of ayre, and doing nothing else since they sat.

AUGUST 7TH. I walked homeward and met with Mr. Spong, and he with me as far as the Old Exchange talking of many ingenuous things, musique, and at last of glasses, and I find him still the same ingenuous man that ever he was, and do among other fine things tell me that by his microscope of his owne making he do discover that the wings of a moth is made just as the feathers of the wing of a bird, and that most plainly and certainly. Parted with him, mightily pleased with his company.

AUGUST 13TH. Up, and before I went to the office comes my Taylor with a coate I have made to wear within doors, purposely to come no lower than my knees, for by my wearing a gowne within doors comes all my tenderness about my legs. There comes also Mr. Reeve, with a microscope and scoto-scope. For the first I did give him £5 10s., a great price, but a most curious bauble it is, and he says, as good, nay, the best he knows in England, and he makes the best in the world. The other he gives me, and is of value; and a curious curiosity it is to look objects in a darke room with.

OCTOBER 5TH. So to the Coffee-house, and there fell in dis-course with the Secretary of the Virtuosi of Gresham College, and had very fine discourse with him. He tells me of a new invented instrument to be tried before the College anon, and I intend to see it. So to Trinity House, and there I dined among the old dull fellows, and so home and to my office a while. Thence to the Musique-meeting at the Postoffice, where I was once before. And thither anon come all the Gres-ham College and a great deal of noble company: and the new instrument was brought called the Arched Viall, where being tuned with lute-strings, and played on with kees like an organ, a piece of parchment is always kept moving; and the strings, which by the kees are pressed down upon it, are grated in imitation of a bow, by the parchment; and so it is intended to resemble several vialls played on with one bow, but so basely and harshly that it will never do. But after three hours' stay it could not be fixed in tune; and so they were fain to go to some other musique of instruments.

FEBRUARY 15TH, 1665. To dinner. Thence with Creed to Gresham College, where I had been by Mr. Povy the last week proposed to be admitted a member; and was this day admitted, by signing a book and being taken by the hand by the President, my Lord Brunkard, and some words of admittance said to me. But it is a most acceptable thing to hear their discourse, and see their experiments; which were this day upon the nature of fire, and how it goes out in a place where the ayre is not free, and sooner out where the ayre is exhausted, which they showed by an engine on purpose. After this being done, they to the Crowne Taverne, behind the 'Change, and there my Lord and most of the company to a club supper. Here excellent discourse till ten at night. So home and to bed.

MAY 1ST. By water to Greenwich; and there coaches met us; and to Colonell Blunt's house to dinner. No extraordinary dinner, nor any other entertainment good; but only after dinner to the tryall of several experiments about making of coaches easy. And several we tried; but one did prove mighty easy (not here for me to describe, but the whole body of the coach lies upon one long spring), and we all, one after another, rid in it, and it is very fine and likely to take. These experiments were the intent of their coming, and pretty they are. Thence back by coach to Greenwich, and in his pleasure boat to Deptford, and there stopped and into Mr. Evelyn's, which is a most beautiful place; but it being dark and late, I staid not; but Deane Wilkins and Mr. Hooke and I walked to Redriffe; and noble discourse all day long did please me, and it being late did take them to my house to drink, and did give them some sweetmeats, and thence sent them with a lanthorn home, two worthy persons as are in England, I think, or the world. So to my Lady Batten, where my wife is to-night.

MAY 3RD. Home to dinner, and so out to Gresham College, and saw a cat killed with the Duke of Florence's poyson, and saw it proved that the oyle of tobacco drawn by one of the Society do the same effect, and is judged to be the same thing with the poyson both in colour and smell and effect. I saw also an abortive child preserved fresh in spirits of salt.

JANUARY 22ND, 1666. Presently to the Crowne tavern behind the Exchange by appointment, and there met the first meeting of Gresham College since the plague. Dr. Goddard did fill us with talke; but what, among other fine discourse pleased me most, was about Respiration: that it is not to this day known, or concluded on among physicians, nor to be done either, how the action is managed by nature, or for what use it is. Here late till poor Dr. Merriott was drunk, and so all home, and I to bed.

JULY 29TH (Lord's Day). Home to dinner, where Mr. Spong and Reeves dined with me by invitation. And after dinner to our business of my microscope to be shown some of the observables of that, and then down to my office to looke in a darke room with my glasses and tube, and most excellently things appeared indeed beyond imagination. Thence satisfied exceedingly with all this we home and to discourse many pretty things.

AUGUST 7TH. Up, and to the office, where we sat all the morning, and home to dinner, and then to the office again, being pretty good friends with my wife again. In the evening comes Mr. Reeves, with a twelve-foote glasse, so I left the office and home, where I met Mr. Batelier with my wife, in order to our going to-morrow, by agreement, to Bow to see a dancing meeting. But, Lord! to see how soon I could conceive evil fears and thoughts concerning them; so Reeves and I and they up to the top of the house, and there we endeavoured to see the moon, and Saturne and Jupiter; but the heavens proved cloudy, and so we lost our labour, having taken pains to get things together, in order to the managing of our long glasse. So down to supper and then to bed, Reeves lying at my house, but good discourse I had from him in his own trade, concerning glasses.

AUGUST 8TH. Up, and with Reeves walk as far as the Temple, doing some business in my way at my bookseller's and elsewhere, and there parted, and I took coach, having first discoursed with Mr. Hooke a little, whom we met in the streete, about the nature of sounds, and he did make me understand the nature of musicall sounds made by strings, mighty prettily; and told me that having come to a certain number of vibrations proper to make any tone, he is able to tell how many strokes a fly makes with her wings (those flies that hum in their flying) by the note that it answers to in musique during their flying. That, I suppose, is a little too much refined; but his discourse in general of sound was mighty fine. To my Lady Pooly's, where my wife was with Mr. Batelier and his sisters, and there I found a noble supper. About ten o'clock we rose from the table, and sang a song, and so home in two coaches; and after being examined at Allgate, whether we were husbands and wives, home, and being there come, I find Reeves there, it being a mighty fine bright night, and so upon my leads, though very sleepy, till one in the morning, looking on the moon and Jupiter, with this twelve-foote glasse and

another of six foote, that he hath brought with him to-night, and the sights mighty pleasant, and one of the glasses I will buy, it being very usefull. So to bed mighty sleepy, but with much pleasure. Reeves lying at my house again; and mighty proud I am (and ought to be thankfull to God Almighty) that I am able to have a spare bed for my friends.

NOVEMBER 14TH. Dr. Croone told me, that, at the meeting at Gresham College to-night, which, it seems they now have every Wednesday again, there was a pretty experiment of the blood of one dogg let out, till he died, into the body of another on one side, while all his own run out on the other side. The first died upon the place, and the other very well, and likely to do well. This did give occasion to many pretty wishes, as of the blood of a Quaker to be let into an Archbishop, and such like; but, as Dr. Croone says, may, if it takes, be of mighty use to man's health, for the mending of bad blood by borrowing from a better body.

NOVEMBER 28TH. Mr. Carteret and I to Gresham College, where they meet now weekly again, and here they had good discourse how this late experiment of the dog, which is in perfect good health, may be improved for good uses to men, and other pretty things, and then broke up.

JANUARY 9TH, 1667. To Faythorne, and then to Arundell House, where first the Royall Society meet, by the favour of Mr. Harry Howard, who was there, and has given us his grandfather's library, a noble gift, and a noble favour and undertaking it is for him to make his house the seat for this college. Here was an experiment shown about improving the use of powder for creating of force in winding up of springs and other uses of great worth.

MAY 30TH. Up, and to the office, where all the morning. After dinner I walked to Arundell House, where I find much company, indeed very much company, in expectation of the Duchesse of Newcastle, who had desired to be invited to the Society. Anon comes the Duchesse with her women. Her deportment so ordinary, that I do not like her at all, nor did I hear her say any thing that was worth hearing, but that she was full of admiration, all admiration. Several fine experiments were shown her of colours, loadstones, microscopes, and of liquors: among others, of one that did, while she was there, turn a piece of roasted mutton into pure blood, which was very rare. After they had shown her many experiments, and she cried still she was full of admiration, she departed, being led out and in by several Lords that were there. I by coach home, and there busy at my letters till night, and then with my wife in the evening singing with her in the garden with great pleasure, and so to bed.

NOVEMBER 21ST. Took coach to Arundell House, where the meeting of Gresham College was broke up; but there meeting Creed, I with him to the taverne in St. Clement's Churchyard, where was Deane Wilkins, Dr. Whistler, Dr. Floyd, a divine admitted, I perceive, this day, and other brave men. They discourse of a man that is a little frantic, that hath been a kind of minister, Dr. Wilkins saying that he hath read for him in his church, that is poor and a debauched man, that the College have hired for 20*s.* to have some of the blood of a sheep let into his body; and it is to be done on Saturday next. They purpose to let in about twelve ounces; which, they compute, is what will be let in in a minute's time by a watch. They differ in the opinion they have of the effects of it;

some think it may have a good effect upon him as a frantic man by cooling his blood, others that it will not have any effect at all. But the man is a healthy man, and by this means will be able to give an account what alteration, if any, he do find in himself, and so may be usefull. On this occasion, Dr. Whistler told a pretty story related by Muffet, a good author, of Dr. Caius, that built Keys College; that, being very old, and living only at that time upon woman's milk, he, while he fed upon the milk of an angry, fretful woman, was so himself; and then, being advised to take it of a good-natured, patient woman, he did become so, beyond the common temper of his age. Thus much nutriment, they observed, might do. Their discourse was very fine; and if I should be put out of my office, I do take great content in the liberty I shall be at, of frequenting these gentlemen's company. Broke up thence and home.

NOVEMBER 30TH. Up, and to the office, where all the morning, and then by coach to Arundel House. Here, above all, I was pleased to see the person who had his blood taken out. He speaks well, and did this day give the Society a relation thereof in Latin, saying that he finds himself much better since, and as a new man, but he is cracked a little in his head, though he spoke very reasonably, and very well. He had but 20s. for his suffering it, and is to have the same again tried upon him: the first man that ever had it tried on him in England, and but one that we hear of in France, which was a porter hired by the virtuosos. Here all the afternoon till within night. Saw a pretty deception of the sight by a glass with water poured into it, with a stick standing up with three balls of wax upon it, one distant from the other. How these balls did seem double and disappear one after another, mighty pretty! And so home and tried to make a piece by my ear and viall to "I wonder what the grave," &c., and so to supper and to bed.

MARCH 2ND, 1668. With Lord Brouncker to the Royall Society, where they were just done; but there I was forced to subscribe to the building of a College, and did give £40; and several others did subscribe, but several I saw hang-off; and I doubt it will spoil the Society, for it breeds faction and ill-will, and becomes burdensome to some that cannot or would not do it. Here to my great content I did try the use of the Otacousticon, which was only a great glass bottle broke at the bottom, putting the neck to my eare, and there I did plainly hear the dashing of the oares of the boats in the Thames to Arundell gallery window, which without it I could not in the least do, and may, I believe, be improved to a great height, which I am mighty glad of.

MARCH 12TH. I took my wife up and left her at the 'Change while I to Gresham College, there to shew myself. Here I saw a great trial of the goodness of a burning glass, made of a new figure, not spherical (by one Smithys, I think they call him), that did burn a glove of my Lord Brouncker's from the heat of a very little fire, which a burning glass of the old form, or much bigger, could not do, which was mighty pretty.

JULY 3RD. Betimes to the office. So abroad by water to Eagle Court in the Strand, and there to an alehouse: met Mr. Pierce, the Surgeon, and Dr. Clerke, Waldron, Turberville, my physician for the eyes, and Lowre, to dissect several eyes of sheep and oxen, with great pleasure, and to my great information. But strange that this Turberville should be so great a man, and yet, to this day, hath seen no eyes dissected, or but once, but desired this Dr. Lowre to give him the opportunity to dissect some.

JULY 13TH. This morning I was let blood, and did bleed about fourteen ounces, towards curing my eyes.

JULY 16TH. I by water with my Lord Brouncker to Arundell House, to the Royall Society, and there saw an experiment of a dog's being tied through the back, about the spinal artery, and thereby made void of all motion; and the artery being loosened again, the dog recovers.

## INTERNATIONAL INSULT

NOVEMBER 28TH, 1663. I have been told two or three times, but to-day for certain I am told how in Holland publickly they have pictured our King with reproach. One way is with his pockets turned the wrong side outward, hanging out empty; another with two courtiers picking of his pockets; and a third, leading two ladies, while others abuse him; which amounts to great contempt.

OCTOBER 8TH, 1666. The King hath yesterday in Council declared his resolution of setting a fashion for clothes, which he will never alter. It will be a vest, I know not well how; but it is to teach the nobility thrift, and will do good.

OCTOBER 13TH. To my Lord Bellasses', and he and I together, to White Hall, and there the Duke of York was just come in from hunting. So I stood and saw him dress himself, and try on his vest, which is the King's new fashion, and will be in it for good and all on Monday next, and the whole Court: it is a fashion, the King says, he will never change.

OCTOBER 15TH. This day the King begins to put on his vest, and I did see several persons of the House of Lords and Commons too, great courtiers, who are in it; being a long cassocke close to the body, of black cloth, and pinked with white silke under it, and a coat over it, and the legs ruffled with black ribband like a pigeon's leg; and upon the whole I wish the King may keep it, for it is a very fine and handsome garment.

NOVEMBER 22ND. At noon home to dinner, where my wife and I fell out, I being displeased with her cutting away a lace handkercher sewed about her neck down to her breasts almost, out of a belief, but without reason, that it is the fashion. Here we did give one another the lie too much, but were presently friends, and then I to my office, where very late and did much business, and then home, and there find Mr. Batalier, and did sup and play at cards awhile. But he tells me the newes how the King of France hath, in defiance to the King of England, caused all his footmen to be put into vests, and that the noblemen of France will do the like; which, if true, is the greatest indignity ever done by one Prince to another, and would incite a stone to be revenged; and I hope our King will. This makes me mighty merry, it being an ingenious kind of affront; but yet it makes me angry, to see that the King of England is become so little as to have the affront offered him.

## ENEMY ATROCITIES

T*HE files of any American newspaper from April, 1916, to November, 1918, contain many incidents reminiscent of these below.*—Editor.

February 23rd, 1665. This day, by the blessing of Almighty God, I have lived thirty-two years in the world, and am in the best degree of health at this minute that I have been almost in my life time, and at this time in the best condition of estate that ever I was in—the Lord make me thankfull. Up and to the office, where busy all the morning. At noon to the 'Change, where I hear the most horrid and astonishing newes that ever was yet told in my memory, that De Ruyter with his fleete in Guinny hath proceeded to the taking of whatever we have, forts, goods, ships, and men, and tied our men back to back and thrown them all into the sea, even women and children also. This a Swede or Hamburgher is come into the River and tells that he saw the thing done. But, Lord, to see the consternation all our merchants are in!

February 25th. Up, and to the office, where all the morning. At noon to the 'Change; where just before I come, the Swede that had told the King and the Duke so boldly this great lie of the Dutch flinging our men back to back into the sea at Guinny, so particularly, and readily, and confidently, was whipt round the 'Change: he confessing it a lie, and that he did it in hopes to get something. It is said the Judges, upon demand, did give it their opinion that the law would judge him to be whipt, to lose his eares, or to have his nose slit: but I do not hear that anything more is to be done to him. They say he is delivered over to the Dutch Embassador to do what he pleased with him. But the world to think that there is some design on one side or other, either of the Dutch or French, for it is not likely a fellow would invent such a lie to get money.

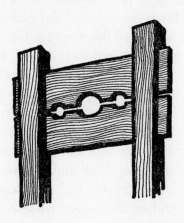

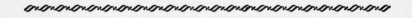

## MR. PEPYS ASSISTS A FRIEND IN TROUBLE

APRIL 3RD, 1664 (Lord's Day). Being weary last night lay long, and called up by W. Joyce. So I rose, and his business was to ask advice of me, he being summonsed to the House of Lords to-morrow, for endeavouring to arrest my Lady Peters for a debt. I did give him advice, and will assist him. He staid all the morning, but would not dine.

APRIL 4TH. Up, and walked to my Lord Sandwich's; and there spoke with him about W. Joyce, who told me he would do what was fit in so tender a point. Thence to Westminster, to the Painted Chamber, and there met the two Joyces. Will in a very melancholy taking. After a little discourse I to the Lords' House before they sat; and stood within it a good while, while the Duke of York came to me. Afterwards I spoke with my Lord Barkeley and my Lord Peterborough about it. And so staid without a good while, and saw my Lady Peters, an impudent jade, soliciting all the Lords on her behalf. And at last W. Joyce was called in; and by the consequences, and what my Lord Peterborough told me, I find that he did speak all he said to his disadvantage, and so was committed to the Black Rod: which is very hard, he doing what he did by the advice of my Lord Peters' own steward. But the Sergeant

of the Black Rod did direct one of his messengers to take him
in custody, and so he was peacably conducted to the Swan
with two Necks, in Tuttle Street, to ? handsome dining-room;
and there was most civilly used, my uncle Fenner, and his
brother Anthony, and some other friends being with him. But
who would have thought that the fellow that I should have
sworn could have spoken before all the world should in this
be so daunted, as not to know what he said, and now to cry
like a child. I protest, it is very strange to observe. I left them
providing for his stay there to-night and getting ready a petition against to-morrow, and so away to Westminster Hall. It
was a sad sight, methought, to-day to see my Lord Peters
coming out of the House fall out with his lady (from whom
he is parted) about this business, saying that she disgraced
him. But she hath been a handsome woman, and is, it seems,
not only a lewd woman, but very high-spirited.

APRIL 5TH. Up very betimes, and walked to my cozen
Anthony Joyce's, and thence with him to his brother Will, in
Tuttle Street, where I find him pretty cheery over he was
yesterday (like a coxcomb), his wife being come to him, and
having had his boy with him last night. Here I staid an hour
or two and wrote over a fresh petition, that which was drawn
by their solicitor not pleasing me, and thence to the Painted
chamber, and by and by away by coach to my Lord Peterborough's, and there delivered the petition into his hand,
which he promised most readily to deliver to the House to-day.
Thence back, and there spoke to several Lords, and so did his
solicitor (one that W. Joyce hath promised £5 to if he be
released). Lord Peterborough presented a petition to the House
from W. Joyce; and a great dispute, we hear, there was in the

House for and against it. At last it was carried that he should be bayled till the House meets again after Easter, he giving bond for his appearance. This was not so good as we hoped, but as good as we could well expect. Thence, after the House was up, I to W. Joyce, with his brother, and told them all. I would not stay to dinner, thinking to go home to dinner, and did go by water as far as the bridge, but thinking they would take it kindly my being there, to be bayled for him if there was need, I returned, but finding them gone out to look after it, only Will and his wife and sister left and some friends that came to visit him, I to Westminster Hall, whither I sent for a lobster. After staying there 3 or 4 hours, I went to W. Joyce, where I find the order come, and bayle (his father and brother) given; and he paying his fees, which come to above £12, besides £5 he is to give one man, and his charges of eating and drinking there, and 10s. a-day for as many days as he stands under bayle: which, I hope, will teach him hereafter to hold his tongue better than he used to do. Thence with Anth. Joyce's wife alone home talking of Will's folly.

APRIL 18TH. Up and by coach to Westminster, and there solicited W. Joyce's business again; and did speak to the Duke of Yorke about it, who did understand it very well. I afterwards did without the House fall in company with my Lady Peters, and endeavoured to mollify her; but she told me she would not, to redeem her soul from hell, do anything to release him; but would be revenged while she lived, if she lived the age of Methusalem. I made many friends, and so did others. At last it was ordered by the Lords that it should be referred to the Committee of Privileges to consider. So I, after discoursing with the Joyces, away.

APRIL 20TH. Up and by coach to Westminster, and there solicited W. Joyce's business all the morning.

APRIL 21ST. Up pretty betimes and to my office. Then comes Mr. Creed, and he and I to Westminster Hall, and there at the Lords' House heard that it is ordered, that, upon submission upon the knee both to the House and my Lady Peters, W. Joyce shall be released. I forthwith made him submit, and aske pardon upon his knees; which he did before several Lords. But my Lady would not hear it; but swore she would post the Lords, that the world might know what pitifull Lords the King hath; and that revenge was sweeter to her than milk; and that she would never be satisfied unless he stood in a pillory, and demand pardon there. But I perceive the Lords are ashamed of her.

APRIL 26TH. I went and saw W. Joyce, and by and by comes in Anthony, they both owning a great deal of kindness received from me in their late business, and indeed I did what I could, and yet less I could not do. It has cost the poor man above £40; besides, he is likely to lose his debt. Thence to my Lord's, and by and by he comes down, and with him (Creed with us) I rode in his coach to St. James's, talking about W. Joyce's business mighty merry, and my Lady Peters, he says, is a drunken jade, he himself having seen her drunk in the lobby of their House.

## STRANGE AND MARVELLOUS

JANUARY 16TH, 1662. At night to Sir W. Batten, and there saw him and Captain Cock and Stokes. Stokes told us, that notwithstanding the country of Gambo is so unhealthy, yet the people of the place live very long, so as the present king there is 150 year old, which they count by rains: because every year it rains continually four months together. He also told us, that the kings there have above 100 wives a-piece, and offered him the choice of any of his wives to lie with, and so he did Captain Holmes. So home and to bed.

FEBRUARY 4TH. At noon to my Lord Crew's where one Mr. Templer (an ingenious man and a person of honour he seems to be) dined; and, discoursing of the nature of serpents, he told us some that in the waste places of Lancashire do grow to a great bigness, and that do feed upon larks, which they take thus:—They observe when the lark is soared to the highest, and so crawl till they come to be just underneath them; and there they place themselves with their mouths uppermost, and there, as is conceived, they do eject poyson up to the bird; for the bird suddenly come down again in its course of a circle, and falls directly into the mouth of the serpent; which is very strange. He is a great traveller, and speaking of the tarantula, he says that all the harvest long (about which times they are most busy) there are fidlers go up and down the fields everywhere, in expectation of being hired by those that are stung.

SEPTEMBER 5TH. Among other pretty discourse, some was of Sir Jerom Bowes, Embassador from Queene Elizabeth to the Emperor of Russia; who, because some of the noblemen there would go up the stairs to the Emperor before him, he would not go up until the Emperor had ordered these two men to be dragged down-stairs, with their heads knocking on every stair till they were killed. And when he was come up, they demanded his sword of him before he entered the room. He told them, if they would have his sword, they should have his boots too. And so caused his boots to be pulled off, and his night-gown and night-cap and slippers to be sent for; and made the Emperor stay till he could go in his night-dress, since he might not go as a soldier. And lastly, when the Emperor in contempt, to show his command of his subjects, did command one to leap from the window down and broke his neck in the sight of our Embassador, he replied that his mistress did set more by, and did make better use of the necks of her subjects: but said that, to show what her subjects would do for her, he would, and did, fling down his gantlett before the Emperor; and challenged all the nobility there to take it up, in defence of the Emperor against his Queen: for which, at this very day, the name of Sir Jerom Bowes is famous and honoured there.

JUNE 15TH, 1663. Anon we sat down to dinner, which was very great. Mr. Prin, among many, had a pretty tale of one that brought in a bill in parliament for the impowering him to dispose his land to such children as he should have that should bear the name of his wife. It was in Queen Elizabeth's time. One replied that there are many species of creatures where the male gives the denomination to both sexes, as swan and woodcock, but not above one where a female do, and that is a goose. Both at and after dinner we had great discourses of the nature and power of spirits, and whether they can animate dead bodies; in all which, as of the general appearance, my Lord Sandwich is very scepticall. He says the greatest warrants that ever he had to believe any, is the present appearance of the Devil in Wiltshire, much of late talked of, who beats a drum up and down. There are books of it, and, they say, very true; but my Lord observes, that though he do answer to any tune that you will play to him upon another drum, yet one tune he tried to play and could not; which makes him suspect the whole; and I think it is a good argument.

NOVEMBER 11TH. Dribble the German Doctor do offer an instrument to sink ships; he tells me that which is more strange, that something made of gold, which they call in chymistry *Aurum fulminans,* a grain, I think he said, of it put into a silver spoon and fired, will give a blow like a musquett, and strike a hole through the spoon downward, without the least force upward; and this he can make a cheaper experiment of, he says, with iron prepared.

FEBRUARY 1ST, 1664. In my way home I 'light and to the Coffee-house, where I heard Lt. Coll. Baron tell very good stories of his travels over the high hills in Asia above the clouds, how clear the heaven is above them, how thick like a mist the way is through the cloud that wets like a sponge one's clothes, the ground above the clouds all dry and parched, and nothing in the world growing, it being only a dry earth, yet not so hot above as below the clouds. The stars at night most delicate bright and a fine clear blue sky, but cannot see the earth at any time through the clouds, but the clouds look like a world below you.

SEPTEMBER 16TH. Met Mr. Pargiter, and he would needs have me drink a cup of horse-radish ale, which he and a friend of his troubled with the stone have been drinking of, which we did and then walked into the fields as far almost as Sir G. Whitmore's, all the way talking of Russia, which he says, is a sad place; and, though Moscow is a very great city, yet it is from the distance between house and house, and few people compared with this, and poor, sorry houses, the Emperor himself living in a wooden house, his exercise only flying a hawk at pigeons and carrying pigeons ten or twelve miles off and then laying wagers which pigeon shall come soonest home to her house. All the winter within doors, some few playing at chesse, but most drinking their time away. Women live very slavishly there, and it seems in the Emperor's court no room hath above two or three windows, and those the greatest not a yard wide or high, for warmth in winter time, and that the general cure for all diseases there is their sweating houses, or people that are poor they get into their ovens, being heated, and there lie. Little learning among things of any sort. Not a man that speaks Latin, unless the Secretary of State by chance.

AUGUST 17TH. Back with Captain Erwin, discoursing about the East Indys, where he hath often been. And among other things he tells me how the King of Syam seldom goes out without thirty or forty thousand people with him, and not a word spoke, nor a hum or cough in the whole company to be heard. He tells me the punishment frequently there for malefactors is cutting off the crowne of their head, which they do very dexterously, leaving their brains bare, which kills them presently. He told me what I remember he hath once done heretofore: that everybody is to lie flat down at the coming of the King, and nobody to look upon him upon pain of death. And that he and his fellows, being strangers, were invited to see the sport of taking a wild elephant, and they did only kneel, and look toward the King. Their druggerman did desire them to fall down, for otherwise he should suffer for their contempt of the King. The sport being ended, a messenger comes from the King, which the druggerman thought he had been sent to have taken away his life. But it was to enquire how the strangers liked the sport. The druggerman answered that they did cry it up to be the best that ever they saw, and that they never heard of any Prince so great in everything as this King. The messenger being gone back, Erwin and his company asked their druggerman what he had said, which he told them. But why, say they, would you say that without our leave, it being not true? "It is no matter for that," says he, "I must have said it, or have been hanged, for our King do not live by meat, nor drink, but by having great lyes told him."

SEPTEMBER 21ST, 1668. To Southwarke-Fair, and there saw the puppet-show of Whittington, which was very pretty to see; and how that idle thing to work upon people that see it, and even myself too! And thence to Jacob's Hall's dancing on the ropes, where I saw such action as I never saw before, and mightily worth seeing; and here took acquaintance with a fellow that carried me to a tavern, whither come the musick of this booth, and by and by Jacob Hall himself, with whom

I had a mind to speak, to hear whether he had ever any mischief by falls in his time. He told me, "Yes, many; but never to the breaking of a limb:" he seems a mighty strong man. So giving them a bottle or two of wine, I away with Payne, the waterman. He, seeing me at the play, did get a link to light me to the Beare, where Bland, my waterman, waited for me with gold and other things he kept for me, to the value of £40 and more, which I had about me, for fear of my pockets being cut. So by link-light through the bridge, it being mighty dark, but still weather, and so home.

FEBRUARY 23RD, 1669. Up: and to the office, where all the morning, and then home, and put a mouthfull of victuals in my mouth; and by a hackney-coach followed my wife and the girls, who are gone by eleven o'clock, thinking to have seen a new play at the Duke of York's house. But I do find them staying at my tailor's, the play not being to-day, and therefore I now took them to Westminster Abbey, and there did show them all the tombs very finely, having one with us alone, there being other company this day to see the tombs, it being Shrove Tuesday; and here we did see, by particular favour, the body of Queen Katherine of Valois; and I had the upper part of her body in my hands, and I did kiss her mouth, reflecting upon it that I did kiss a Queen, and that this was my birth-day, thirty-six years old, that I did first kiss a Queen. But here this man, who seems to understand well, tells me that the saying is not true that says she was never buried; only, when Henry the Seventh built his chapel, it was taken up and laid in this wooden coffin; but I did there see that, in it, the body was buried in a leaden one, which remains under the body to this day. Thence to the Duke of York's playhouse, and there, finding the play begun, we homeward to the Glass-House, and there shewed my cousins the making of glass, and had several things made with great content; and among others, I had one or two singing-glasses made, which make an echo to the voice, the first that ever I saw; but so thin, that the very breath broke one or two of them.

## MISCELLANY

## FUNDAMENTALS OF HISTORY

MAY 27TH, 1668. To the office, where busy till two o'clock, and then with Sir D. Gawden to his house, with my Lord Brouncker and Sir J. Minnes, to dinner, where we dined very well, and much good company. Thence after dinner to see Sir W. Pen, who I find still very ill of the goute, sitting in his great chair, made on purpose for persons sick of that disease, for their ease; and this very chair, he tells me, was made for my Lady Lambert. And so home, and then made the boy to read to me out of Dr. Wilkins his "Real Character," and particularly about Noah's arke, where he do give a very good account thereof, shewing how few the number of the several species of beasts and fowls were that were to be in the arke, and that there was room enough for them and their food and dung, which do please me mightily and is much beyond what ever I heard of the subject, and so to bed.

145

## ELABORATION ON HAMLET'S SOLILOQUY *

AUGUST 15TH, 1665. Up by 4 o'clock and walked to Greenwich, where called at Captain Cocke's and to his chamber, he being in bed, where something put my last night's dream into my head, which I think is the best that ever was dreamt, which was that I had my Lady Castlemayne in my armes and was admitted to use all the dalliance I desired with her, and then dreamt that this could not be awake, but that it was only a dream; but that since it was a dream, and that I took so much real pleasure in it, what a happy thing it would be if when we are in our graves (as Shakespeere resembles it) we could dream, and dream but such dreams as this, that then we should not need to be so fearful of death, as we are this plague time.

## A STRANGE AND DOUBTFUL DRINK

MARCH 9TH, 1669. With my wife and Bab. and Betty Pepys and W. Hewer, whom I carried all this day with me, to my cozen Stradwick's, where I have not been ever since my brother Tom died, there being some difference between my father and them, upon the account of my cozen Scott; and I was glad of this opportunity of seeing them, they being good and substantial people, and kind, and here, which I never did before, I drank a glass, of a pint, I believe, at one draught, of the juice of oranges, of whose peel they make comfits; and here

* For in that sleep of death what dreams may come
When we have shuffled off this mortal coil
Must give us pause.—*Hamlet,* III, 1.

146

they drink the juice as wine, with sugar, and it is a very fine drink; but, it being new, I was doubtful whether it might not do me hurt. They are very good people. So home, and there after signing my letters, my eyes being bad, to supper and to bed.

## BARBERING AT HOME

MAY 25TH, 1662 (Lord's Day). To trimming myself, which I have this week done every morning, with a pumice stone, which I learnt of Mr. Marsh, when I was last at Portsmouth; and I find it very easy, speedy, and cleanly, and shall continue the practice of it.

MAY 31ST. In a suddaine fit cut off all my beard,* which I had been a great while bringing up, only that I may with my pumice-stone do my whole face, as I now do my chin, and to save time, which I find a very easy way and gentile.

JANUARY 6TH, 1664 (Twelfth Day). This morning I began a practice which I find by the ease I do it with that I shall continue, it saving me money and time; that is, to trimme myself with a razer: which pleases me mightily.

## BARBERING ABROAD

JULY 22ND, 1663. Abroad calling at several places upon some errands, among others to my brother Tom's barber and had my hair cut, while his boy played on the viallin, a plain boy, but has very good genius, and understands the book very well, but to see what a shift he made for a string of red silk was very pleasant. Thence to my Lord Crew's.

* Moustache. Pepys was otherwise smooth-shaven.

## ANTICIPATION AND—

FEBRUARY 20TH, 1665. To the office, and there found Bagwell's wife, whom I directed to go home, and I would do her business, which was to write a letter to my Lord Sandwich for her husband's advance into a better ship as there should be occasion. Which I did. At my office my wife comes and tells me that she hath hired a chamber mayde, one of the prettiest maydes that ever she saw in her life, and that she is really jealous of me for her, but hath ventured to hire her from month to month, but I think she means merrily. So to supper and to bed.

MARCH 6TH. Up, and with Sir J. Minnes by coach, being a most lamentable cold day as any this year, to St. James's, and there did our business with the Duke. Great preparations for his speedy return to sea. I saw him try on his buff coat and hat-piece covered with black velvet. It troubles me more to think of his venture, than of anything else in the whole warr. So home, and there find our new chamber-mayde, Mary, come, which instead of handsome, as my wife spoke and still seems to reckon, is a very ordinary wench, I think, and therein was mightily disappointed.

## ANSWER TO A CLASSIC RIDDLE

DECEMBER 16TH, 1660. With Tom Doling and Boston and D. Vines (whom we met by the way) to Price's, and there we drank, and in discourse I learnt a pretty trick to try whether a woman be a maid or no, by a string going round her head to meet at the end of her nose, which if she be not will come a great way beyond.

## VISITORS FROM THE COUNTRY

APRIL 23RD, 1663. I up betimes, and with my father, having a fire made in my wife's new closet above, it being a wet and cold day, we sat there all the morning looking over his country accounts ever since his going into the country. We resolve upon sending for Will Stankes up to town to give us a right understanding in all that we have in Brampton, and before my father goes to settle everything. To my office and put a few things in order, and so home to spend the evening with my father. At cards till late, and being at supper, my boy being sent for some mustard to a neat's tongue, the rogue staid half an hour in the streets, it seems at a bonfire, at which I was very angry, and resolve to beat him to-morrow.

APRIL 29TH. W. Stankes was come with his horses. But it is very pleasant to hear how he rails at the rumbling and ado that is in London over it is in the country, that he cannot endure it. He supped with us, and very merry, and then he to his lodgings at the Inne with the horses, and so we to bed and both slept very well.

APRIL 30TH. Up, and after drinking my morning draft with my father and W. Stankes, I went forth to my office, where till towards noon: and then to the Exchange, and back home to dinner, where Mrs. Hunt, my father, and W. Stankes; but, Lord! what a stir Stankes makes with his being crowded in the streets and wearied in walking in London, and would not be wooed by my wife and Ashwell to go to a play, nor to White

Hall, or to see the lyons, though he was carried in a coach. I never could have thought there had been upon earth a man so little curious in the world as he is. At the office all the afternoon till 9 at night, so home to cards with my father, wife and Ashwell, and so to bed.

## PERSONAL SANITATION

FEBRUARY 21ST, 1665. My wife with her woman to a hot house to bathe herself, after her long being within doors in the dirt, so that she now pretends to a resolution of being hereafter very clean. How long it will hold I can guess.

FEBRUARY 22ND. Lay last night alone, my wife after her bathinge laying in another bed. So cold all night.

FEBRUARY 25TH. At night late home, and to clean myself with warm water; my wife will have me, because she do herself, and so to bed.

JANUARY 23RD, 1669. To my wife's chamber, and there supped, and got her cut my hair and look my shirt, for I have itched mightily these 6 or 7 days, and when all comes to all she finds that I am lousy, having found in my head and body about twenty lice, little and great, which I wonder at, being more than I have had I believe these 20 years. I did think I might have got them from the little boy, but they did presently look him, and found none. So how they come I know not, but presently did shift myself, and so shall be rid of them, and cut my hair close to my head, and so with much content to bed.

## KEEPING UP WITH THE NEIGHBORS

*In justice to Pepys, be it mentioned that items of this sort are rare in the Diary.*—EDITOR.

MAY 4TH, 1662 (Lord's Day). Lay long talking with my wife. Then Mr. Holliard came to me and let me blood, about sixteen ounces, I being exceedingly full of blood and very good. I begun to be sick; but lying upon my back I was presently well again, and did give him 5s. for his pains, and so we parted, and I, to my chamber to write down my journall from the beginning of my late journey to this house. Dined well, and after dinner, my arm tied up with a black ribbon, I walked with my wife to my brother Tom's; our boy waiting on us with his sword, which this day he begins to wear, to outdo Sir W. Pen's boy, who this day, and Sir W. Batten's too, begin to wear new livery; but I do take mine to be the neatest of them all. When church was done went to Mrs. Turner's, and after a stay there, my wife and I walked to Grays Inn, to observe the fashions of the ladies, because of my wife's making some clothes. Thence homewards.

## A GLIMPSE AT HIGHER EDUCATION

JULY 8TH, 1660 (Lord's Day). Mr. Fairebrother came to call us out to my father's to supper. He told me how he had perfectly procured me to be made Master in Arts by proxy, which did somewhat please me, though I remember my cousin Roger Pepys was the other day persuading me from it.

AUGUST 14TH. Home by water to the Tower, where my father, Mr. Fairbrother, and Cooke dined with me. My father, after dinner, takes leave, after I had given him 40s. for the last half year for my brother John at Cambridge. I did also make even with Mr. Fairbrother for my degree of Master of Arts, which cost me about £9 16s. To White Hall, and my wife with me by water, where at the Privy Seal and elsewhere all the afternoon. At night home with her by water, where I made good sport with having the girl and the boy to comb my head, before I went to bed, in the kitchen.

## MR. PEPYS SEEKS ADVICE

JULY 26TH, 1664. All the morning at the office, at noon to Anthony Joyce's, to our gossip's dinner. I had sent a dozen and a half bottles of wine thither, and paid my double share besides, which is 18s. Very merry we were, and when the women were merry and rose from table, I above with them, ne'er a man but I, I began discourse of my not getting of children, and prayed them to give me their opinions and advice, and they freely and merrily did give me these ten, among them—(1) Do not hug my wife too hard nor too much; (2) eat no late suppers; (3) drink juyce of sage; (4) tent and toast; (5) wear cool holland drawers; (6) keep stomach warm and back cool; (7) upon query whether it was best to do at night or morn, they answered me neither one nor the other, but when we had most mind to it; (8) wife not to go too straight laced; (9) myself to drink mum and sugar; (10) Mrs. Ward did give me, to change my place. The 3rd, 4th, 6th, 7th, and 10th they all did seriously declare, and lay much stress on them as rules fit to be observed indeed, and especially the last, to lie with our heads where our heels do, or at least to make the bed high at feet and low at head.

## REMEDIES FOR DISTRESS

APRIL 3RD, 1661. Up among my workmen, my head akeing all day from last night's debauch. To the office all the morning, and dined with Sir W. Batten and Pen, who would needs have me drink two drafts of sack to-day to cure me of last night's disease, which I thought strange, but I think find it true.

APRIL 24TH. Waked in the morning with my head in a sad taking through last night's drink which I am very sorry for; so rose and went out with Mr. Creed to drink our morning draft, which he did give me in chocolate to settle my stomach.

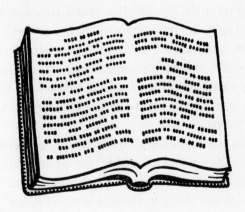

# THE FOUNDER OF PENNSYLVANIA

JANUARY 25TH, 1662. At home and the office all the morning. Walking in the garden to give the gardener directions what to do this year (for I intend to have the garden handsome), Sir W. Pen came to me, and did break a business to me about removing his son from Oxford to Cambridge to some private college. I proposed Magdalene, but cannot name a tutor at present; but I shall think and write about it.

APRIL 28TH, 1662. Sir W. Pen much troubled upon letters came last night. Showed me one of Dr. Owen's to his son, whereby it appears his son is much perverted in his opinion by him; which I now perceive is one thing that hath put Sir William so long off the books. By coach to the Pay-house, and so to work again, and so in the evening to the yard, and supper and bed.

JULY 5TH. To my office all the morning, to get things ready against our sitting, and by and by we sat and did business all the morning, and at noon had Sir W. Pen, who I hate with all my heart for his base treacherous tricks, but yet I think it not policy to declare it yet, and his son William, to my house to dinner.

AUGUST 26TH, 1664. This day my wife tells me Mr. Pen, Sir William's son, is come back from France, and come to visit her. A most modish person, grown, she says, a fine gentleman.

AUGUST 30TH. To dinner at home; after dinner comes Mr. Pen to visit me, and staid an houre talking with me. I perceive something of learning he hath got, but a great deale, if not too much, of the vanity of the French garbe, and affected manner of speech and gait. I fear all real profit he hath made of his travel will signify little. So, he gone, I to my office and there very busy.

DECEMBER 29TH, 1667 (Lord's Day). At night comes Mrs. Turner to see us; and tells me that Mr. William Pen, who is lately come over from Ireland, is a Quaker again, or some very melancholy thing; that he cares for no company, nor comes into any: which is a pleasant thing, after his being abroad so long, and his father such a hypocritical rogue, and at this time an Atheist. She gone, I to my very great content do find my accounts to come very even and naturally, and so to supper and to bed.

OCTOBER 12TH, 1668. At my house staid and supped, and this night my bookseller Shrewsbury comes, and brings my books of Martyrs, and I did pay him for them, and did this night make the young woman before supper to open all the volumes for me. So to supper, and after supper to read a ridiculous nonsensical book set out by Will. Pen, for the Quakers; but so full of nothing but nonsense, that I was ashamed to read in it. So they gone, we to bed.

FEBRUARY 12TH, 1669. To Dancre's, and there saw our picture of Greenwich in doing, which is mighty pretty, and so

to White Hall, my wife to Unthank's, and I attended with
Lord Brouncker the King and Council, about the proposition
of balancing storekeeper's accounts. Thence I homeward, and
calling my wife, called at my cozen Turner's, and there met
our new cozen Pepys (Mrs. Dickenson), and Bab. and Betty
come yesterday to town, poor girls, whom we have reason
to love, and mighty glad we are to see them; and there staid
and talked a little, being also mightily pleased to see Betty
Turner, who is now in town, and her brothers Charles and
Will, being come from school to see their father, and there
talked a while and so home, and there Pelling hath got me
W. Pen's book against the Trinity. I got my wife to read it
to me; and I find it so well writ as, I think, it is too good for
him ever to have writ it; and it is a serious sort of book, and
not fit for every body to read. So to supper and to bed.

## ON THE VANITY OF WOMAN

NOVEMBER 4TH, 1660 (Lord's Day). My wife seemed very pretty to-day, it being the first time I have given her leave to wear a black patch.

NOVEMBER 22ND. Mr. Fox did receive us with a great deal of respect; and then did take my wife and I to the Queen's presence-chamber, where he got my wife placed behind the Queen's chair, and I got into the crowd, and by and by the Queen and the two Princesses came to dinner. The Queen a very little plain old woman, and nothing more in her presence in any respect nor garb than any ordinary woman. The Princess of Orange I had often seen before. The Princess Henrietta is very pretty, but much below my expectation; and her dressing of herself with her hair frized short up to her ears, did make her seem so much the less to me. But my wife standing near her with two or three black patches on, and well dressed, did seem to me much handsomer than she.

MARCH 8TH, 1664. Up with some little discontent with my wife upon her saying that she had got and used some puppy-dog water, being put upon it by a desire of my aunt Wight to get some for her, who hath a mind, unknown to her husband, to get some for her ugly face. I to the office.

MAY 28TH, 1667. After dinner my wife away down with Jane and W. Hewer to Woolwich, in order to a little ayre and to lie there to-night, and so to gather May-dew to-morrow morning, which Mrs. Turner hath taught her as the only thing in the world to wash her face with; and I am contented with it. Presently comes Creed, and he and I by water to Fox-hall, and there walked in Spring Garden. A great deal of company, and the weather and garden pleasant: that is very pleasant and cheap going thither, for a man may go to spend what he will, or nothing, all is one. But to hear the nightingale and the other birds, and here fiddles, and there a harp, and here a Jew's trump, and here laughing, and there fine people walking, is mighty divertising. Among others, there were two pretty women alone, that walked a great while, which being discovered by some idle gentlemen, they would needs take them up; but to see the poor ladies how they were put to it to run from them, and they after them, and sometimes the ladies put themselves along with other company, then the other drew back; at last, the last did get off out of the house, and took boat and away. I was troubled to see them abused so, and could have found in my heart, as little desire of fighting as I have, to have protected the ladies. So by water, set Creed down at White Hall, and I to the Old Swan, and so home.

MAY 5TH, 1668. Up, and all the morning at the office. At noon home to dinner and Creed with me, and after dinner he and I to the Duke of York's playhouse; and there coming late, he and I up to the balcony-box, where we find my Lady Castlemayne and several great ladies. One thing of familiarity I observed in my Lady Castlemayne: she called to one of her women for a little patch off her face, and put it into her mouth and wetted it, and so clapped it upon her own by the side of her mouth, I suppose she feeling a pimple rising there.

## MY WIFE, POOR WRETCH!

AUGUST 18TH, 1660. This morning I took my wife towards Westminster by water, and landed her at Whitefriars, with £5 to buy her a petticoat, and I to the Privy Seal. By and by comes my wife to tell me that my father has persuaded her to buy a most fine cloth of 26*s.* a yard, and a rich lace, that the petticoat will come to £5, at which I was somewhat troubled, but she doing it very innocently, I could not be angry. I did give her more money, and sent her away, and I dined at the Leg in King Street.

OCTOBER 24TH. I lay and slept long to-day. I took occasion to be angry with my wife before I rose about her putting up of half a crown of mine in a paper box, which she had forgot where she had lain it. But we were friends again as we are always.

OCTOBER 24TH, 1662. After with great pleasure lying a great while talking and sporting in bed with my wife (for we have been for some years now, and at present more and more, a very happy couple, blessed be God), I got up and to my office. So home and dined there with my wife upon a most excellent dish of tripes of my own directing, covered with mustard, as I have heretofore seen them done at my Lord Crew's.

JUNE 11TH, 1663. At night home and spent the evening with my wife, and she and I did jangle mightily about her cushions that she wrought with worsteds the last year, which are too little for any use, but were good friends by and by again. But one thing I must confess I do observe, which I did not before, which is, that I cannot blame my wife, for I am taken up in my talk with Ashwell, who is a very witty girl, that I am not so fond of her as I used and ought to be, which now I do perceive I will remedy, but I would to the Lord I had never taken any, though I cannot have a better than her.

JUNE 15TH. Up betimes, and anon my wife rose and did give me her keys, and put other things in order and herself against going this morning into the country. I was forced to go to Thames Street, and after her to her inn, where I am troubled to see her forced to sit in the back of the coach, though pleased to see her company none but women and one parson; she I find is troubled at all, and I seemed to make a promise to get a horse and ride after them; and so, kissing her often, and Ashwell once, I bid them adieu. Up to my wife's closett and there played on my viallin a good while, and without supper anon to bed, sad for want of my wife, whom I love with all my heart, though of late she has given me some troubled thoughts.

JULY 5TH (Lord's Day). Lady Batten had sent twice to invite me to go with them to Walthamstow to-day, Mrs. Martha being married this morning to Mr. Castle. A good dinner and merry, but methinks none of the kindness nor bridall respect between the bridegroom and bride that was between my wife and I.

DECEMBER 19TH, 1664. Going to bed betimes last night we waked betimes, and from our people's being forced to take the key to go out to light a candle, I was very angry and begun to find fault with my wife for not commanding her servants as she ought. Thereupon, she giving me some cross answer, I did strike her over her left eye such a blow as the poor wretch did cry out and was in great pain, but yet her spirit was such as to endeavour to bite and scratch me. But I coying with her made her leave crying, and sent for butter and parsley, and friends presently one with another, and I up, vexed at my heart to think what I had done, for she was forced to lay a poultice or something to her eye all day, and is black, and the people of the house observed it. But I was forced to rise, and up and with Sir J. Minnes to White Hall, and there we waited on the Duke. Thence home, and not finding Bagwell's wife as I expected, I to the 'Change and there walked up and down, and then home, and she being come I bid her go and stay at Mooregate for me, and after going up to my wife (whose eye is very bad, but she is in very good temper to me), and after dinner I to the place and walked round the fields again and again, but not finding her I to the 'Change, and there found her waiting for me and took her away, and to an alehouse, and there made I much of her, and then away thence and to another and endeavoured to caress her, but elle ne voulait pas,* which did vex me, but I think it was chiefly not having a good easy place to do it upon.

FEBRUARY 25TH, 1667. Lay long in bed, talking with pleasure with my poor wife, how she used to make coal fires, and wash my foul clothes with her own hand for me, poor wretch!

* She did not want to.

in our little room at my Lord Sandwich's; for which I ought for ever to love and admire her, and do; and persuade myself she would do the same thing again, if God should reduce us to it.

MARCH 1ST. So to the office till dinner-time, and then home to dinner, and before dinner making my wife to sing. Poor wretch! her ear is so bad that it made me angry, till the poor wretch cried to see me so vexed at her, that I think I shall not discourage her so much again, but will endeavour to make her understand sounds, and do her good that way; for she hath a great mind to learn, only to please me; and, therefore, I am mighty unjust to her in discouraging her so much, but we were good friends, and to dinner, and had she not been ill with those and that it were not Friday (on which in Lent there are no plays) I had carried her to a play, but she not being fit to go abroad, I to the office.

MARCH 5TH. Up, and to the office, where met and sat all the morning, doing little for want of money, but only bear the countenance of an office. Then to see Sir W. Batten, whose leg is all but better than it was. I by discourse do perceive he and his Lady are to their hearts out with my Lord Bruncker and Mrs. Williams, to which I added something, but, I think, did not venture too far with them. But, Lord! to see to what a poor content any acquaintance among these people, or the people of the world, as they now-a-days go, is worth; for my part, I and my wife will keep to one another and let the world go hang. So home to supper and hear my wife and girle sing a little, and then to bed with much content of mind.

MARCH 27TH, 1668. Home to dinner, where my wife and I had a small squabble, but I first this day tried the effect of my silence and not provoking her when she is in an ill humour, and do find it very good, for it prevents its coming to that height on both sides which used to exceed what was fit between us. So she become calm by and by and fond.

## MR. PEPYS FEELS GUILTY

FEBRUARY 11TH, 1667. After walking a good while in the Hall [Westminster], it being Term time, I home by water, calling at Michell's and giving him a fair occasion to send his wife to the New Exchange to meet my wife and me this afternoon. So home to dinner, and after dinner by coach to Lord Bellasses'. Having done what we had to do there, my Lord carried me and set me down at the New Exchange, where I staid at Pottle's shop till Betty Michell come, which she did about five o'clock, and was surprised not to trouver * my muger there; but I did make an excuse good enough, and so I took elle down, and over the water to the cabinet-maker's, and there bought a dressing-box for her for 20s., but would require an hour's time to make fit. The mistresse of the shop took us into the kitchen and there talked and used us very prettily, and took her for my wife, which I owned and her big belly, and there very merry till my thing done, and then took coach and home. But now comes our trouble, I did begin to fear that su marido might go to my house to enquire

* *Trouver*, find; *muger*, wife; *elle*, her; *su marido*, her husband; *pour*, for; *trouvant*, finding; *femme*, wife; *je allois con elle*, I went with her; *su*, his; *tergo de her mari*, back of her husband; *la cose*, the matter; *ante*, before; *à my femme*, to my wife; *su donna*, her mistress.

pour elle, and there, trouvant my muger at home, would not only think himself, but give my femme occasion to think strange things. This did trouble me mightily, so though elle would not seem to have me trouble myself about it, yet did agree to the stopping of the coach at the streete's end, and je allois con elle home, and there presently hear by him that he had newly sent su mayde to my house to see for her mistresse. This do much perplex me, and I did go presently home (Betty whispering me behind the tergo de her mari, that if I would say that we did come home by water, elle could make up la cose well satis), and there in a sweat did walk in the entry ante my door, thinking what I should say à my femme, and as God would have it, while I was in this case (the worst in reference à my femme that ever I was in my life), a little woman comes stumbling to the entry steps in the dark; whom asking who she was, she enquired for my house. So knowing her voice, and telling her su donna is come home she went away. But, Lord! in what a trouble was I, when she was gone, to recollect whether this was not the second time of her coming, but at last concluding that she had not been here before, I did bless myself in my good fortune in getting home before her, and do verily believe she had loitered some time by the way, which was my great good fortune, and so in a-doors and there find all well. So my heart full of joy, I to the Office a while and then home, and after supper and doing a little business in my chamber I to bed, after teaching Barker a little of my song.

*In about a month, Mr. Pepys had more than recovered from his fright.*—EDITOR.

# Samuel Pepps' Diarp

MARCH 13TH. To Westminster Hall, and there met Doll
Lane coming out, and par contrat* did hazer bargain para
aller to the cabaret de vin, called the Rose, and ibi I staid two
hours, sed she did not venir, lequel troubled me, and so away
by coach and took up my wife, and away home, and so to Sir
W. Battens.

* *Par contrat*, by agreement; *hazer*, make; *para aller*, to go; *cabaret de vin*,
wine shop; *ibi*, thither; *sed*, but; *venir*, come; *lequel*, which.

〜〜〜〜〜〜〜〜〜〜〜〜〜〜〜〜〜〜〜〜〜〜〜〜

## THE DIARIST IN CHURCH

JANUARY 8TH, 1660 (Sunday). In the morning I went to Mr. Gunning's, where a good sermon, wherein he shewed the life of Christ, and told us good authority for us to believe that Christ did follow his father's trade, and was a carpenter till thirty years of age. From thence to my father's to dinner, where I found my wife, who was forced to dine there, we not having one coal of fire in the house. In the afternoon my wife and I went to Mr. Mossum's where a strange doctor made a very good sermon.

*Between the above date and the next, King Charles II was restored, and public worship turned toward the "high" church.*
—EDITOR.

JULY 1ST. Dined at home alone. In the afternoon to the Abbey, where a good sermon by a stranger, but no Common Prayer yet.

JULY 8TH (Lord's Day). To White Hall Chapel, where I got in with ease by going before the Lord Chancellor with Mr. Kipps. Here I heard very good music, the first time that ever I remember to have heard the organs and singing-men in surplices in my life. The Bishop of Chichester preached before the King, and made a great flattering sermon, which I did not like that Clergy should meddle with matters of state. Dined with Mr. Luellin, and Salisbury, at a cook's shop.

OCTOBER 4TH. To Whitehall, and from thence I and Lieut. Lambert to Westminster Abbey, where we saw Dr. Frewen translated to the Archbishoprick of York. Here I saw the Bishops of Winchester, Bangor, Rochester, Bath and Wells, and Salisbury, all in their habits, in King Henry Seventh's chappell. But Lord! at their going out, how people did most of them look upon them as strange creatures, and few with any kind of love or respect.

NOVEMBER 4TH (Lord's Day). In the morn to our own church, where Mr. Mills did begin to nibble at the Common Prayer, by saying, "Glory be to the Father, &c." after he had read the two psalms; but the people had been so little used to it, that they could not tell what to answer. After dinner to the Abbey, where the first time that ever I heard the organs in a cathedral.

FEBRUARY 17TH, 1661 (Lord's Day). A most tedious, unreasonable, and impertinent sermon by an Irish Doctor. His text was "Scatter them, O Lord, that delight in war." Sir Wm. Batten and I very much angry.

NOVEMBER 17TH (Lord's Day). So to Church again, and heard a simple fellow upon the praise of Church musique, and exclaiming against men's wearing their hats on in the church, but I slept part of the sermon, till latter prayer and blessing and all was done, without waking, which I never did in my life.

MAY 25TH, 1662 (Lord's Day). To church, and heard a good sermon of Mr. Woodcocke's at our church; only in his latter prayer for a woman in childbed, he prayed that God would deliver her from the hereditary curse of child-bearing, which seemed a pretty strange expression. Dined at home, and Mr. Creed with me.

AUGUST 17TH (Lord's Day). Up very early, this being the last Sunday that the Presbyterians are to preach, unless they read the new Common Prayer, and renounce the Covenant, and so I had a mind to hear Dr. Bates's farewell sermon, and so walked to St. Dunstan's, where, it not being seven o'clock yet, the doors were not open; and so I went and walked an hour in the Temple-garden, reading my vows, which it is a great content to me to see how I am a changed man in all respects for the better, since I took them, which the God of Heaven continue to me, and make me thankful for. At eight o'clock I went, and crowded in at a back door among others, the church being half-full almost before any doors were open publicly; which is the first time that I have done so these many years since I used to go with my father and mother, and so got into the gallery, beside the pulpit, and heard very well. His text was, "Now the God of Peace——;" the last Hebrews, and the 20th verse: he making a very good sermon, and very little reflection in it to anything of the times. After dinner to St. Dunstan's again; and the church quite crowded before I came.

APRIL 5TH, 1663 (Lord's Day). To dinner and very well pleased with it. Then to church again, where a simple bawling young Scot preached.

JUNE 21ST (Lord's Day). So to church, and slept all the sermon, the Scot, to whose voice I am not to be reconciled, preaching.

OCTOBER 14TH. My wife and I, by Mr. Rawlinson's conduct, to the Jewish Synagogue: where the men and boys in their vayles, and the women behind a lattice out of sight; and some things stand up, which I believe is their Law, in a press to which all coming in do bow, and at the putting on their vayles do say something, to which others that hear him do cry Amen, and the party do kiss his vayle. Their service all in a singing way, and in Hebrew. And anon their Laws that they take out of the press are carried by several men, four or five several burthens in all, and they do relieve one another; and whether it is that every one desires to have the carrying of it, I cannot tell, thus they carried it round about the room while such a service is singing. And in the end they had a prayer for the King, which they pronounced his name in Portugall; but the prayer, like the rest, in Hebrew. But, Lord! to see the disorder, laughing, sporting, and no attention, but confusion in all their service, more like brutes than people knowing the true God, would make a man forswear ever seeing them more: and indeed I never did see so much, or could have imagined there had been any religion in the whole world so absurdly performed as this.

DECEMBER 27TH. Up and to church alone, and so home to dinner. After dinner to the French church, but came too late, and so back to our owne church, where I slept all the sermon, to Scott preaching, and so home.

AUGUST 18TH, 1667 (Lord's Day). I walked towards White Hall, but, being wearied, turned into St. Dunstan's Church, where I heard an able sermon of the minister of the place; and stood by a pretty, modest maid, whom I did labour to take by the hand and the body; but she would not, but got further and further from me; and at last I could perceive her take pins out of her pocket to prick me if I should touch her again—which seeing I did forbear, and was glad I did spy her design. And then I fell to gaze upon another pretty maid in a pew close to me, and she on me; and I did go about to take her by the hand, which she suffered a little and then withdrew. So the sermon ended, and the church broke up, and my amours ended also, and so took coach and home, and there took up my wife.

## SURGERY AND CELEBRATION

MARCH 26TH, 1660. This day it is two years since it pleased God that I was cut of the stone at Mrs. Turner's in Salisbury Court. And did resolve while I live to keep it a festival, as I did the last year at my house, and for ever to have Mrs. Turner and her company with me. But now it pleases God that I am where I am [*He was at sea, on business.*—EDITOR.] and so prevented to do it openly; only within my soul I can and do rejoice.

MARCH 26TH, 1661. Up early and to do business in my study. This is the great day that three years ago I was cut of the stone, and, blessed be God, I do yet find myself very free from pain again. All this morning I staid at home looking after my workmen to my great content about my stairs, and at noon by coach to my father's, where Mrs. Turner, The., Joyce, Mr. Morrice, Mr. Armiger, Mr. Pierce, the surgeon, and his wife, my father and mother, and myself and my wife. Very merry at dinner; among other things, because Mrs. Turner and her company eat no flesh at all this Lent, and I had a great deal of good flesh which made their mouths water.

MARCH 26TH, 1662. Up early. This being, by God's great blessing, the fourth solemn day of my cutting for the stone this day four years, and am by God's mercy in very good health, and like to do well, the Lord's name be praised for it. At noon come my good guests, Madame Turner, The., and cozen Norton, and a gentleman, one Mr. Lewin of the King's Life Guard; by the same token he told us of one of his fellows killed this morning in a duel. I had a pretty dinner for them, viz., a brace of stewed carps, six roasted chickens, and a jowl of salmon, hot, for the first course; and a tanzy and two neats' tongues, and cheese the second; and were very merry all the afternoon, talking and singing and piping upon the flageolette. In the evening they went with great pleasure away, and I with great content and my wife walked half an hour in the garden, and so home to supper and to bed.

JANUARY 27TH, 1663. I have news this day from Cambridge that my brother hath had his bachelor's cap put on; but that which troubles me is, that he hath the pain of the stone, and makes bloody water with great pain, it beginning just as mine did. I pray God help him.

FEBRUARY 27TH. Up and to my office, whither several persons came to me about office business. About 11 o'clock, Commissioner Pett and I walked to Chyrurgeon's Hall (we being all invited thither, and promised to dine there); where we were led into the Theatre; and by and by comes the reader, Dr. Tearne, with the Master and Company, in a very handsome manner; and all being settled, he begun his lecture, this being the second upon the kidneys, ureters, &c., which was very fine; and his discourse being ended, we walked into the Hall, and there being great store of company, we had a fine dinner and good learned company, many Doctors of Physique, and we used with extraordinary great respect. [*Later*] We went into a private room, where I perceive they prepare the bodies, and there were the kidneys, ureters [&c.], upon which he read to-day, and Dr. Scarborough upon my desire and the company's did show very clearly the manner of the disease of the stone and the cutting and all other questions that I could think of.

APRIL 4TH. Up betimes and to my office. I returned home to dinner, whither by and by comes Roger Pepys, Mrs. Turner her daughter, Joyce Norton, and a young lady, a daughter of Coll. Cockes, my uncle Wight, his wife and Mrs. Anne Wight. This being my feast, in lieu of what I should have had a few days ago for my cutting of the stone, for which the Lord make me truly thankful. Very merry at, before, and after dinner, and the more for that my dinner was great, and most neatly dressed by our own only maid. We had a fricasee of rabbits and chickens, a leg of mutton boiled, three carps in a dish, a great dish of a side of lamb, a dish of roasted pigeons, a dish of four lobsters, three tarts, a lamprey pie (a most rare pie), a dish of anchovies, good wine of several sorts, and all things mighty noble and to my great content. After dinner to Hide Park.

MAY 30TH. Up betimes, and so my brother's, and there I found my aunt James, a poor, religious, well-meaning, good soul, talking of nothing but God Almighty, and that with so much innocence that mightily pleased me. Here was a fellow that said grace so long like a prayer; I believe the fellow is a cunning fellow, and yet I by my brother's desire did give him a crown, he being in great want, and, it seems, a parson among the fanatiques, and a cozen of my poor aunt's, whose prayers she told me did do me good among the many good souls that did by my father's desires pray for me when I was cut of the stone, and which God did hear, which I also in complaisance did own; but, God forgive me, my mind was otherwise. She going out of town to-day, and being not willing to come home with me to dinner, I parted and home.

MARCH 26TH, 1664. Up very betimes and to my office. Home and there found Madam Turner, her daughter The., Joyce Norton, my father and Mr. Honywood, and by and by come my uncle Wight and aunt. This being my solemn feast for my cutting of the stone, it being now, blessed be God! this day six years since the time, and I bless God I do in all respects find myself free from that disease or any signs of it, more than that upon the least cold I continue to have pain in making water, by gathering of wind and growing costive, till which be removed I am at no ease. Ended the day with great content to think how it has pleased the Lord in six years time to raise me from a condition of constant and dangerous and most painfull sicknesse and low condition and poverty to a state of constant health almost, great honour and plenty, for which the Lord God of Heaven make me truly thankfull.

JUNE 1ST. Mr. Hollyard came to me and to my great sorrow, after his great assuring me that I could not possibly have the stone again, he tells me that he do verily fear that I have it again, and has brought me something to dissolve it, which do make me very much troubled and pray to God to ease me. By appointment met my wife, and she and I to the King's house, and saw "The Silent Woman"; but methought not so well done or so good a play as I formerly thought it to be, or else I am now-a-days out of humour. Before the play was done, it fell such a storm of hayle, that we in the middle of the pit were fain to rise; and all the house in a disorder, and so my wife and I out and got into a little ale house, and staid there an hour after the play was done before we could get a coach.

AUGUST 19TH. Creed came to me, and he and I out, among other things, to look out a man to make a case for to keep my stone, that I was cut of, in, but I missed of my end.

AUGUST 20TH. I forth to bespeak a case to keep my stone in, which will cost me 25*s*.

SEPTEMBER 16TH. I forth with my boy to buy severall things, and walked to the mathematical instrument maker in Moore-fields and bought a large pair of compasses, and there met Mr. Pargiter, and he would needs have me drink a cup of horse-radish ale, which he and a friend of his troubled with the stone have been drinking of, which we did and then walked into the fields as far almost as Sir G. Whitmore's, all the way talking of Russia, which, he says, is a sad place.

MARCH 26TH, 1665 (Lord's Day and Easter Day). Up (and with my wife, who has not been at church a month or two) to church. At noon home to dinner, my wife and I (Mercer staying to the Sacrament) alone. This is the day seven years which, by the blessing of God, I have survived of my being cut of the stone, and am now in very perfect good health and have long been; and though the last winter hath been as hard a winter as any have been these many years, yet I never was better in my life, nor have not, these ten years, gone colder in the summer than I have done all this winter, wearing only a doublet, and a waistcoate cut open on the back; abroad, a cloake and within doors a coate I slipped on. Now I am at a losse to know whether it be my hare's foot which is my preservative against wind, for I never had a fit of the collique since I wore it, and nothing but wind brings me pain, and the carrying away of wind takes away my pain, or my keeping my back cool; for when I do lie longer than ordinary upon my back in bed, my water the next morning is very hot, or whether it be my taking of a pill of turpentine every morning, which keeps me always loose, or all together, but this I know, with thanks to God Almighty, that I am now as well as ever I can wish or desire to be, having now and then a little pain, but it is over presently, only I do find that my backe grows very weak.

MARCH 26TH, 1667. Up with a sad heart in reference to my mother, of whose death I undoubtedly expect to hear the next post; but on my own behalf I have cause to be joyful this day, it being my usual feast day, for my being cut of the stone this day nine years, and through God's blessing am at this day and have long been in as good condition of health as ever I was in my life or any man in England is, God make me thankful for it! But the condition I am in, in reference to my mother, makes it unfit for me to keep my usual feast.

APRIL 30TH. Up, and Mr. Madden come to speak with me. Then comes Sir John Winter to discourse with me about the forest of Deane, and then about my Lord Treasurer, and asking me whether, as he had heard, I had not been cut for the stone, I took him to my closet, and there shewed it to him, of which he took the dimensions and had some discourse of it, and I believe will show my Lord Treasurer it. Thence to the office.

MAY 3RD. I presently to the Excise Office, and there met the Cofferer and [Sir] Stephen Fox by agreement, and then we three to my Lord Treasurer, who continues still very ill. I had taken my stone with me on purpose, and Sir Philip Warwicke carried it in to him to see, but was not in a condition to talk with me about it, poor man. I to Westminster Hall, and there took a turn with my old acquaintance Mr. Pechell, whose red nose, makes me ashamed to be seen with him, though otherwise a good-natured man.

## A SERIOUS MATTER

JUNE 12TH, 1666. Up, and to the office, where we sat all the morning. At noon to dinner, and then to White Hall, in hopes of a meeting. Walking there in the galleries I find the Ladies of Honour dressed in their riding garbs, with coats and doublets with deep skirts, just for all the world like mine, and buttoned their doublets up the breast, with perriwigs and with hats; so that, only for a long petticoat dragging under their men's coats, nobody could take them for women in any point whatever, which was an odde sight, and a sight did not please me. It was Mrs. Wells and another fine lady that I saw thus.

AUGUST 14TH (Thanksgiving Day). Home and dined, and after dinner with my wife and Mercer to the Beare-garden, where I have not been, I think, of many years, and saw some good sport of the bull's tossing of the dogs, one into the very boxes. But it is a very rude and nasty pleasure. Thence home, well enough satisfied, however, with the variety of this afternoon's exercise; and so I to my chamber, till in the evening our company come to supper. We had invited to a venison pasty Mr. Batelier and his sister Mary, Mrs. Mercer, her daughter Anne, Mr. Le Brun, and W. Hewer; and so we supped, and very merry. And then about nine o'clock to Mrs. Mercer's gate, where the fire and boys expected us, and her son had provided abundance of serpents and rockets; and there mighty merry (my Lady Pen and Pegg going thither with us, and Nan Wright), till about twelve at night, flinging our fireworks, and burning one another and the people over the way. And at last our businesses being most spent, we into Mrs. Mercer's, and there mighty merry, smutting one another with candle-grease and soot, till most of us were like devils. And that being done, then we broke up, and to my house; and there I made them drink; and upstairs we went, and then fell into dancing (W. Batelier dancing well) and dressing, him and I and one Mr. Banister (who with his wife come over also with us) like women; and Mercer put on a suit of Tom's, like a boy, and mighty mirth we had, and Mercer danced a jigg; and Nan Wright and my wife and Pegg Pen put on perriwigs. Thus we spent till three or four in the morning, mighty merry; and then parted, and to bed.

~~~~~~~~~~~~~~~~~~~~~~~~~~~~~~~~~~~~~~~~~~~~~~~~~~~

## MR. PEPYS LAMENTS THE HIGH COST OF LIVING

*EIGHT days after the entry below, our gentleman esti-
mated his wealth at £650, besides goods of all sorts.
See the item of December 31st, 1662, in "Stages of
Affluence, and Some Sources."—*EDITOR.

DECEMBER 23RD, 1662. And slept hard till 8 o'clock this
morning, and so up and to the office, and at noon home to
dinner with my wife alone, and after dinner sat by the fire,
and then up to make up my accounts with her, and find that
my ordinary housekeeping comes to £7 a month, which is a
great deal.

*Since then, Mr. Pepys's estate has more than trebled.—*
EDITOR.

OCTOBER 11TH, 1665. Up, and so in my chamber staid all the
morning doing something toward my Tangier accounts, for
the stating of them, and also comes up my landlady, Mrs.
Clerke, to make an agreement for the time to come; and I,
for the having room enough, and to keepe out strangers, and
to have a place to retreat to for my wife, if the sicknesse

should come to Woolwich, am contented to pay dear; so for three rooms and a dining-room, and for linen and bread and beer and butter, at nights and mornings, I am to give her £5 10s. per month.

MAY 12TH, 1667 (Lord's Day). Against noon we had a coach ready for us, and [my wife] and I to White Hall, where I went to see whether Sir G. Carteret was at dinner or no, our design being to make a visit there, and I found them set down, which troubled me, for I would not then go up, but back to the coach to my wife, and she and I homeward again. And in our way bethought ourselves of going alone, she and I, to go to a French house to dinner, and so enquired out Monsieur Robins, my perriwigg-maker, who keeps an ordinary, and in an ugly street in Covent Garden did find him at the door, and so we in; and in a moment almost had the table covered, and clean glasses, and all in the French manner, and a mess of potage first, and then a couple of pigeons à la esterve, and then a piece of bœuf-à-la-mode, all exceedingly well seasoned, and to our great liking; at least it would have been anywhere else but in this bad street, and in a periwigg-maker's house; but to see the pleasant and ready attendance that we had, and all things so desirous to please, and ingenious in the people, did take me mightily. Our dinner cost us 6s., and so my wife and I away to Islington, it being a fine day, and thence to Sir G. Whitmore's house, where we 'light, and walked over the fields to Kingsland, and back again; a walk, I think, I have not taken these twenty years; but puts me in mind of my boy's time when I boarded at Kingsland, and used to shoot with my bow and arrows in these fields. A very pretty place it is; and little did any of my friends think I should come to walk in these fields in this condition and state that I am. Then took coach again, and home through Shoreditch.

JANUARY 4TH, 1669. Lay long, talking with my wife, and did of my own accord come to an allowance of her of £30 a-year for all expences, clothes and everything, which she was mightily pleased with, it being more than ever she asked or expected, and so rose, with much content, and up with W. Hewer to White Hall. Took up my wife at Unthank's, and so home, and there with pleasure to read and talk, and so to supper, and put into writing, in merry terms, our agreement between my wife and me, about £30 a-year, and so to bed. This was done under both our hands merrily, and put into W. Hewer's to keep.

## MR. PEPYS SEEKS TREASURE

OCTOBER 30TH, 1662. Could sleep but little tonight for thoughts of my business. So up by candlelight and by water to Whitehall, and so to my Lord Sandwich, who was up in his chamber and all alone, did acquaint me with his business; which was, that our old acquaintance Mr. Wade (in Axe Yard) hath discovered to him £7,000 hid in the Tower, of which he was to have two for discovery; my Lord himself two, and the King, the other three, when it was found; and that the King's warrant runs for me on my Lord's part, and one Mr. Lee for Sir Harry Bennett, to demand leave of the Lieutenant of the Tower for to make search. After he had told me of the whole business, I took leave and hastened to my office, expecting to be called by a letter from my Lord to set upon the business. At noon comes Mr. Wade with my Lord's letter. After dinner, Sir H. Bennett did call aside the Lord Mayor and me, and did break the business to him. Mr. Wade and one Evett his guide did come, and W. Griffin, and a porter with his picke-axes, &c.; and my Lord Mayor did give us full power to fall to work. So our guide demands a candle, and down into the cellars he goes. We went into several little cellars; but none did answer so well to the marks which was given

him to find it by, as one arched vault. Where, after a great deal
of council whether to set upon it now, or delay for better and
more full advice, we set to it, to digging we went to almost
eight o'clock at night, but could find nothing. But, however,
our guides did not at all seem discouraged; for that they being
confident that the money is there they look for, but having
never been in the cellars, they could not be positive to the
place, and therefore will inform themselves more fully now
they have been there of the party that do advise them. So we
left work tonight.

NOVEMBER 1ST. To my office; sent for to meet Mr. Leigh
again, from Sir. H. Bennett. And he and I, with Wade and
his intelligencer and labourers, to the Tower cellars, to make
one tryall more; where we staid two or three hours digging,
and dug a great deal all under the arches, as it was now most
confidently directed, and so seriously, and upon pretended
good grounds, that I myself did truly expect to speed; but we
missed of all, and so we went away the second time like fools.
Mr. Leigh goes home to Whitehall; and I by appointment to
the Dolphin Tavern, to meet Wade and the other, Capt.
Evett, who now do tell me plainly, that he that do put him
upon this is one that had it from Barkestead's own mouth, and
was advised with by him, just before the King's coming in,
how to get it out, and had all the signs told him how and
where it lay, and had always been the great confident of
Barkestead even to the trusting him with his life and all he
had. So that he did much convince me that there is good
ground for what we go about. But I fear it may be that he
did find some conveyance of it away, without the help of this

man, before he died. But he is resolved to go to the party once more, and then to determine what we should do further.

NOVEMBER 3RD. At night to my office, and did business; and there came to me Mr. Wade and Evett, who have been again with their prime intelligencer, a woman, I perceive: and though we have missed twice, yet they bring such an account of the probability of the truth of the thing, though we are not certain of the place, that we shall set upon it once more; and I am willing and hopefull in it. So we resolved to set upon it again on Wednesday morning; and the woman herself will be there in disguise, and confirm us in the place.

NOVEMBER 7TH. Up and being by appointment called upon by Mr. Lee, he and I to the Tower, to make our third attempt upon the cellar. And now privately the woman, Barkestead's great confident, is brought, who do positively say that this is the place which he did say the money was hid in, and where he and she did put up the £50,000 [*How this has multiplied!* —EDITOR.] in butter firkins; and the very day that he went out of England did say that neither he nor his would be the better for that money, and therefore wishing that she and hers might. And so left us, and we full of hope did resolve to dig all over the cellar, which by seven o'clock at night was per-formed. At noon we sent for a dinner, and upon the head of a barrel dined very merrily, and to work again. Between times Mr. Lee, who had been much in Spain, did tell me pretty stories of the customs and other things, as I asked him, of the country, to my great content. But at last we saw we were mis-taken; and after digging the cellar quite through and remov-ing the barrels from one side to the other, we were forced to pay our porters, and give over our expectations, though I do believe there must be money hid somewhere by him, or else he did delude this woman in hopes to oblige her to further serving him, which I am apt to believe. Thence by coach to White Hall, and at my Lord's lodgings did write a letter, he not being within, to tell him how things went.

## *REQUIESCAT IN PACE*

MARCH 15TH, 1664. About eight o'clock my brother began to fetch his spittle with more pain, and to speak as much but not so distinctly. I had no mind to see him die, as we thought he presently would, and so withdrew and led Mrs. Turner home, but before I came back, which was in half a quarter of an hour, my brother was dead. I went up and found the nurse holding his eyes shut, and he poor wretch lying with his chops fallen, a most sad sight, and that which put me in a present very great transport of grief and cries, and indeed it was a most sad sight to see the poor wretch lie now still and dead, and pale like a stone. I staid till he was almost cold, while Mrs. Croxton, Holden and the rest did strip him and lay him out, they observing his corpse, as they told me afterwards, to be as clear as any they ever saw, and so this was the end of my poor brother. I left my wife to see him laid out, and I by coach home carrying my brother's papers, all I could find, with me, and having wrote a letter to my father I returned by coach, it being very late, and dark, to my brother's, but all being done, the corpse laid out, and my wife at Mrs. Turner's, I thither, and there after an hour's talk, we up to bed.

MARCH 16TH. And then I rose, and up, leaving my wife in bed, and to my brother's, where I set them on cleaning the house, and my wife coming anon to look after things, I up and down to my cozen Stradwicke's and uncle Fenner's about discoursing for the funeral, which I am resolved to put off till Friday next. So I left them, and to my brother's to look after things, and saw the coffin brought. At last, I to Mrs. Turner's, and there, though my heart is still heavy to think of my poor brother, yet I could give way to my fancy to hear Mrs. The. play upon the Harpsicon, though the musique did not please me neither. Thence to my brother's and found them with my mayd Elizabeth taking an inventory of the goods of the house, which I was well pleased at, and am much beholden to Mr. Honeywood's man in doing it.

MARCH 17TH. Up and to my brother's, where all the morning doing business against to-morrow, and so to my cozen Stradwicke's about the same business, and so to the office. After office I to my brother's again, and thence to Madam Turner's, in both places preparing things against to-morrow; and this night I have altered my resolution of burying him in the churchyarde among my young brothers and sisters, and resolve to bury him in the church, in the middle aisle, as near as I can to my mother's pew. This costs me 20s. more. This being all, home by coach, bringing my brother's silver tankard for safety along with me, and so to supper, after writing to my father, and so to bed.

MARCH 18TH. Up betimes, and walked to my brother's, where a great while putting things in order against anon; then to Madam Turner's, and eat a breakfast there, and so to Wotton my shoemaker, and there got a pair of shoes blacked on the soles against anon for me; so to my brother's and to church, and with the grave-maker chose a place for my brother to lie in, just under my mother's pew. But to see how a man's tombes are at the mercy of such a fellow that for sixpence he would, (as his owne words were,) "I will justle them together but I will make room for him;" speaking of the fulness of the middle isle, where he was to lie; and that he would, for my father's sake, do my brother that is dead all the civility he can; which was to disturb other corps that are not quite rotten, to make room for him; and methought his manner of speaking it was very remarkable; as of a thing that now was in his power to do a man a courtesy or not. At noon my wife comes, but I being forced to go home, she went back with me, where I dressed myself, and so did Besse; and so to my brother's again: whither, though invited, as the custom is, at one or two o'clock, they came not till four or five. But at last one after another they come, many more than I bid: and my reckoning that I bid was one hundred and twenty; but I believe there was nearer one hundred and fifty. Their service was six biscuits a-piece, and what they pleased of burnt claret. My cosen Joyce Norton kept the wine and cakes above; and did give out to them that served, who had white gloves given them. But above all I am beholden to Mrs. Holden, who was most kind, and did take mighty pains not only in getting the house and every thing else ready, but this day in going up and down to see the house filled and served, in order to mine, and their great content, I think; the men sitting by themselves in some rooms, and women by themselves in others, very close, but yet room enough. Anon to church, walking out into the streete to the Conduit, and so across the streete, and had a very good company along with the corps. And being come to the grave as above, Dr. Pierson, the minister of the parish, did read the service for buriall: and so I saw my poor brother laid into the grave; and so all broke up; and I and my wife and Madam Turner and her family to my brother's, and by and by fell to a barrell of oysters, cake and cheese, of Mr. Honiwood's, with him, in his chamber and below, being too merry for so late a sad work. But, Lord! to see how the world makes nothing of the memory of a man, an houre after he is dead! And indeed, I must blame myself; for though at the sight of him dead and dying, I had real grief, yet presently after, and ever since, I have had very little grief indeed for him. By and by home to supper and to bed.

## THE LAST ENTRY IN THE DIARY

MAY 31ST, 1669. Up very betimes, and so continued all the morning with W. Hewer, upon examining and stating my accounts, in order to the fitting myself to go abroad beyond sea, which the ill conditions of my eyes, and my neglect for a year or two, hath kept me behindhand in, and so as to render it very difficult now, and troublesome to my mind to do it; but I this day made a satisfactory entrance therein. Dined at home, and in the afternoon by water to White Hall, calling by the way of Michell's, where I have not been many a day till just the other day, and now I met her mother there and knew her husband to be out of town. And here je did baiser elle,* but had not opportunity para hazer some with her as I would have offered if je had had it. And thence had another meeting with the Duke of York, at White Hall, on yesterday's work, and made a good advance: and so, being called by my wife, we to the Park, Mary Batelier, and a Dutch gentleman, a friend of hers, being with us. Thence to "The World's End," a drinking-house by the Park; and there merry, and so home late.

\* *Je* did *baiser elle*—I did kiss her; *para hazer,* to do.

And thus ends all that I doubt I shall ever be able to do with my own eyes in the keeping of my Journal, I being not able to do it any longer, having done now so long as to undo my eyes almost every time that I take a pen in my hand; and, therefore, whatever comes of it I must forbear: and, therefore, resolve, from this time forward, to have it kept by my people in long-hand, and must therefore be contented to set down no more than is fit for them and all the world to know; or if there be any thing, which cannot be much, now my amours to Deb. are past, and my eyes hindering me in almost all other pleasures, I must endeavour to keep a margin in my book open, to add, here and there, a note in short-hand with my own hand.

And so I betake myself to that course, which is almost as much as to see myself go into my grave: for which, and all the discomforts that will accompany my being blind, the good God prepare me!

S.P.

MAY 31, 1669

# Samuel Pepys' Diary

## INDEX

# INDEX

# Index

# Index

# Index

## T

Tangier business, investigation of, 86-91
   profits from, 71, 72, 74, 76, 79
Tearne, Dr., 176
Telescope, 121
Templer, Mr., 138
Theatre-going, 37, 53, 112, 114, 143, 158, 178
Thurlow, Secretary, 15
Tobacco oyle experiments, 121
Tom, uncle, 17
Tooker, Mrs., 110
Treasure-hunt, 187-192
Turberville, Dr., 128
Turner, Betty, 38, 156
Turner, Charles, 156
Turner, Mrs., 80, 82, 112, 151, 155, 158, 194
   Pepys's gratitude to, 175-181
Turner, The, at Pepys's celebrations, 175-178
Turner, Will, 156

## V

Vaughan, Mr., 90
Vines, Dick, 76, 148
Vows, 65, 172

## W

Wade, Mr., treasure hunt, 187-191
Waldron, Mr., 128
Warren, Sir W., 70, 114
Water-drawing engines, 116
Weaver, Mrs., 37
Westminster Abbey, 143, 171
Whistler, Dr., 78, 126, 127
Wight, aunt, 157, 177
Wight, uncle, 177
Wight, Mrs. Anne, 177
"Wild Goose Chase, The," 37
Wilkins, Deane, 120, 126, 145
Willet, Deborah, 112
   service in the house of Mr. Pepys, 35-59
Williams, Mrs., 110
Winter, Sir John, 180
Woodcocke, Mr., 171
Wright, Lady, 97, 99

## Y

York, Duke of, 41, 44, 52, 57, 74, 114, 134, 136
   dress of, 130
   praise of Pepys, 84, 89
Young, Mr., 78